'... between two evils, I refuse to choose the lesser.' Karl Kraus, quoted in Pierre Bourdieu, *Acts of Resistance. Against the New Myths of our Time* (Cambridge: Polity Press, 1998) 8-9

# CULTURAL ACTIVISM TODAY.
## The Art of Over-Identification

BAVO (editors) / episode publishers, Rotterdam 2007

# Introduction: Cultural Activism Today.
# The Art of Over-Identification

by BAVO

In 2002, Santiago Sierra made a land artwork, in which he had African day labourers dig out three thousand holes of precise dimensions in a tight, geometric grid on a Spanish slope facing the coast of Morocco, paying them the minimum wage stipulated by the Spanish government: € 54 for eight hours of work. This work is entitled 3000 holes 180 x 50 x 50 cm each. Like a true capitalist, Sierra simply sat down, did nothing, took some photographs and consumed the surplus value that was generated at the expense of the day labourers. In 1999, he pulled the same stunt by paying some unemployed Cuban youngsters to have a line tattooed on their backs for the ridiculous amount of $ 30 each. The title of this work is 250 cm line tattooed on 6 paid people. In a similar vein, artist Jens Haaning, in an action in a Swiss contemporary art centre in 1998, waged a true price war with local supermarkets by selling all kinds of goods for up to 35% cheaper by cleverly abusing the differential import taxes for art objects between France and Switzerland. This action took place in the Centre for Contemporary Art in Fribourg (Switzerland). Think also of Haaning's earlier work Trade Bartering (1996), in which he sold goods imported as art objects from Denmark in an art centre in Oslo, enabling him to beat the nearest competitor by up to 40%.

These works are exemplary of a certain tendency in contemporary art, in which artists, faced by a world that is more than ever ruled by a calculating cynicism, strategically give up their will to resist, capitulate to the status quo and apply the latter's rules even more consistently and scrupulously than the rest of society. In doing so, they provoke by asking why should art be an exception when it comes to ruthlessly exploiting cheap labour for self-enrichment (Sierra) or manipulating one's monopoly position to outdo the competition (Haaning). In other words, they ask why art cannot be as nakedly self-interested and capitalist as everything else in the 'real' world.

This volume of essays, which is the outcome of a symposium held in Amsterdam in January 2006, theoretically explores this strategy of over-identification as an effective means of artistic resistance today. We speak of over-identification, since the artists in question strategically over-identify with the ruling norms and practices instead of con- testing them or inventing an alternative for them, which would be characteristic of the critical and utopian art strategies respectively.

The main thrust of Cultural Activism Today. The Art of Over-Identification is that the latter strategies have become increasingly ineffective, since it conforms to what is expected – demanded even – of artists, that is, to relentlessly and idealistically confront society with its shortcomings or to propose 'other' ideals capable of rejuvenating society. Elsewhere we spoke of the artist as 'subject supposed to subvert'. BAVO, 'The Spectre of the Avant-Garde. Contemporary Reassertions of the Programme of Subversion in Cultural Production', in: Andere Sinema 176 (2006) 24-41. This societal demand is, in fact, a bogus one, since art's critical or utopian mandate is simultaneously limited by the constant warning that its activity should remain realistic and especially constructive. Such constructive criticism is, of course, nothing but a coded way of saying that it should not question or undermine the win-win combination of representative democracy and free market economy – the two 'golden calves' of this self-acclaimed age of the end of history. If artists do get carried away by their iconoclastic or revolutionary enthusiasm, they are immediately accused of regressing into backward, totalitarian forms of society, preaching anarchy or even paving the way for terrorism.

By radically refusing this role of the 'last of the idealists', which, so we contend, enforces all kinds of self-limitations and self-censorship on artists and is nothing but a farce anyway, the art of over-identification offers an uneasy answer to the question of artistic resistance 'after' the end of history. It asks of artists to ignore society's pathetic demand for small creative acts and, inversely, to uncompromisingly identify with the ruling order itself and to act out its logic in its most extreme, dystopian form. To be sure, confronting society in this way with its own closure demands of artists to stop being the good guy who protects society from what it wants or offers it some artistic relief – as should be clear by the actions of Sierra and Haaning referred to above. Instead, they should turn society into the worst version of itself in order to confront it with the impossibility of its desire. The aim of this strategy of over-identification should thus be clear: by sabotaging society's tendency to delegate its task of resistance to the safe haven of art, it no longer grants society any escape from its own, immanent laws, but forces it to start subverting itself.

In what follows, we shall give a brief summary of the different contributions to this volume that all analyse, in one way or another, the art of over-identification.

Our contribution sets out and contextualizes the problematics of this book. It starts by sketching the post-critical condition in which artists have to operate today. Against the current tendency of what we call NGO art, which aims at making the world a slightly better place through artistic interventions, we claim that artists should rather make it worse, adding fuel to the fire so as to radically confront the current order with the ultimate consequences of its own principles. With the aid of the documentary *The Yes Men* and an artistic action by Christoph Schlingensief we elaborate upon some of the fundamental principles of the art of over-identification.

In his essay, Alexei Monroe focuses on the motif of the stag in the work of the 'fathers of over-identification': *Neue Slowenische Kunst*. He claims that cultural agents should not stick to a *cordon sanitaire* when it comes to symbols that at first sight seem reactionary – like the stag. On the contrary, in the knowledge that many of these symbols actually contain contradictory meanings and origins, they should, according to Monroe, fully identify with them in such a way as to channel their often powerfully mythical significations for progressive purposes.

Benda Hofmeyr deals with the recent work of the Dutch art collective Atelier Van Lieshout (AVL) such as *SlaveCity*, that over-identifies with an inconsistent mix of contemporary ideological formations such as deep ecology, flexible capitalism and high tech. In the concentration camp-like environment that results from this, she sees an application of Foucault's definition of critique in terms of 'how not to be governed'. However, the subversive potential of the contradictory enjoyment that AVL's works produce in their audience is, according to Hofmeyr, threatened due to the lack of seriousness and political intentionality with which it is put forward.

Dieter Lesage's contribution critically investigates the strategy of over-identification in two recent projects by architect Rem Koolhaas: his so-called 'barcode flag' for the EU and his design for the Prada shop in New York. He claims that these respective identifications with the EU and creative capitalism lack any subversive potential since they fail to question the basic presuppositions of capitalist liberal democracy. Lesage further deals with the strategy of overstatement as applied in *Documenta* 11. Again, he reveals how the overstating of *Documenta* 11's allegiance with anti- and otherglobalist resistance movements, is based on a deeper attitude of acceptance and resignation towards the status quo.

Finally, Boris Groys pleas for the over-identification with the artistic avant-garde's struggle for equal aesthetic rights. He sees the latter threatened by the current pseudo-democratization of image production by the mass media. For him, this development is, in fact, nothing but a regression to premodernity, since it leads to the creation of new icons and idols. In unleashing a new iconoclasm, so he claims, artists should not be afraid to take an elitist or undemocratic approach, even reinstating the place of the museum as the last bulwark or, put better, the first outpost in the struggle to demystify today's seemingly real and autonomous image production.

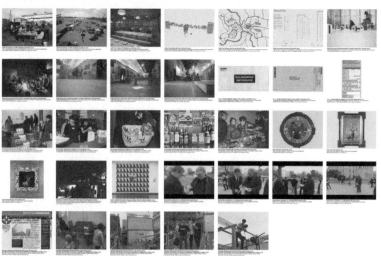

**Christoph Schlingensief, *Bitte liebt Österreich!*, action, Vienna (2002),
still taken from Paul Poet's documentary *Ausländer Raus. Schlingensief's Container* (2005)**
*Big Brother* show in which the Austrian people could vote asylum seekers off the
show and out of the country. *Copyright: Monitorpop Entertainment*

**Irwin, *Vade Retro*, mixed media (1988)**
Series of icons in which the symbol of the stag is juxtaposed
with modernist motifs. *Photo and copyright: Irwin*

**Michael Moore, *Fahrenheit 9/11*, still taken from the movie (2004)**
Pro-war U.S. congressmen are encouraged to set a good example by sending
their sons and daughters to Iraq. Copyright: Lionsgate Films

12 – Cultural Activism Today. The Art of Over-Identification

**Molly Nesbit, Hans-Ulrich Obrist, Rirkrit Tiravanija, *Utopia Station*, curatorial project, 50th Venice Biennale (2003)** Artworks are used by the curators as illustrations and documents of their vision of utopia. *Photo and copyright: Studio Armin Linke*

**Atelier Van Lieshout, *Slave City*, mixed media (2005)**
A forced labour camp for 200,000 inmates combining state of the art technological innovation with the latest management skills for maximum profit. *Photo and copyright: Atelier Van Lieshout*

Christoph Schlingensief, *Bitte liebt Österreich!*, action, Vienna (2002), still taken from Paul Poet's documentary *Ausländer Raus. Schlingensief's Container* (2005) *Big Brother* show in which the Austrian people could vote asylum seekers off the show and out of the country. Copyright: Monitorpop Entertainment

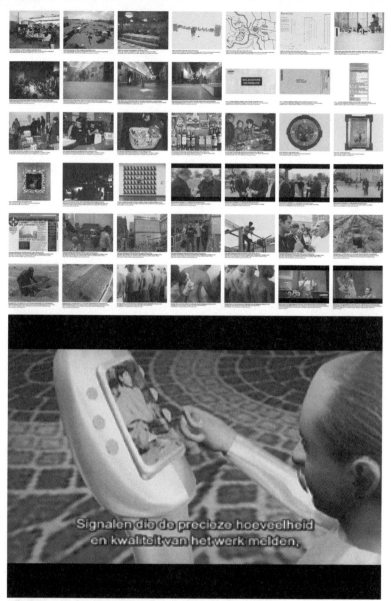

Mike Bonanno and Andy Bichlbaum, *The Yes Men*, action, still taken from the movie directed by among others Dan Ollman (2003) Two anti-corporate activists lecturing on the latest developments in labour disciplining at an economic forum, posing as representatives of the WTO.

**Jens Haaning, *Trade Bartering*, installation, Kunstnernes Hus, Oslo (1996)**
By importing consumer items from Denmark to Norway as art objects, visitors could acquire the goods up to 40 % cheaper. *Photo and copyright: Jens Haaning*

# Always Choose the Worst Option.
## Artistic Resistance and the Strategy
## of Over-Identification
by BAVO

Introduction: Shut Up and Give Us Art!

As a protest against the upsurge of extreme right sentiments in his home country Switzerland and its impact upon democracy, artist Thomas Hirschhorn occupied the Swiss Cultural Centre in Paris for several days in 2005. There he staged an anarchistic show that levelled a withering critique against Swiss domestic politics, questioning its democratic character and mocking elements from popular culture that are manipulated by politicians and the media to propagate racist policies. Hirschhorn's action was entitled Swiss Swiss Democracy and took place in the Centre Culturel du Suisse in Paris, March 2005. It followed his earlier boycott against performing in Switzerland since October 2003 when Christopher Blocher, the leader of the Swiss Populist Party UDC was appointed Minister of Justice and Police. Needless to say, it did not take long for the politicians in question to strike back. The latter accused Hirschhorn of not respecting the democratic rules of the game, of using illegitimate means to manipulate public opinion, and of exceeding the extent of his power and expertise as an artist. In the end, this led to the Swiss parliament's decision to reduce the budget of the Pro Helvetia foundation that subsidized Hirschhorn's action.

This is exemplary of the sad fate of art in our current social order. On the one hand, art is seen as one of democracy's most essential pillars: it is the space *par excellence* for the free expression of ideas, the experimentation with new models of society. However, when an artist takes this role too seriously and becomes too straightforwardly political, s/he is accused of demagogy or simply discarded as bad art. In short, s/he receives the same frosty treatment as the country rock band The Dixie Chicks did after having made the fatal error of uttering a word of criticism against G.W. Bush's war on Iraq. The underlying message of the organized boycotts of the band and public destruction of their records was loud and clear: 'shut up and sing' – as the title of the documentary rightly suggests – i.e. as artists, they should stick to what they know. It is clear that art is here defined in the most narrow, regressive way possible – as a specialized, politically neutral discipline focused on the production of beautiful objects or, in the case of The Dixie Chicks, beautiful sounds. The trouble started for the Dixie Chicks when, during a concert in London, the lead singer admitted to the audience to be ashamed to come from Texas 'too', which was immediately interpreted by a lot of Americans as a sign of being unpatriotic and as support for terrorists. *See documentary* Shut up and Sing *(Cabin Creek Films, 2006), directed by Barbara Kopple and Cecila Peck.*

This condescending treatment of art is the suffocating fate we all – artists or not – face today in these post-political times. On the one hand, one is allowed to say everything, experiment with everything, and criticize everything. More than allowed, it is expected, *demanded* even as our civic, democratic duty. Still, if one takes this commandment to subvert and criticize too far or too seriously – and 'too far' today means that one fundamentally questions the ideological coordinates of the current order such as representative democracy, the free market or the nation-state – one is immediately disqualified as a legitimate discussion partner, treated like an incompetent, ignorant imbecile who stepped out of line and should better stick to his own field of expertise. Needless to say, such reasoning could not be further removed from democratic politics proper, which, according to political philosopher Jacques Rancière, precisely takes place when somebody makes a claim that s/he is unauthorized or unqualified to do. *See Jacques Rancière, La Mésentente. Politique et philosophie (Paris: Galilée, 1995).* It is precisely this 'stepping out of line' that is foreclosed in the situation described above by sticking to a strongly hierarchized image of society in which politics is regarded as a specialized field of expertise populated by political professionals who are the sole masters of the art of politics.

Today's Blackmail of Constructive Critique

One of the most symptomatic manifestations of this onslaught on any real critique, i.e. critique that does not limit itself to mere window dressing, is no doubt today's insistence on constructive critique. What has become completely unacceptable is to 'merely' criticize, that is, to critically diagnose and analyse society's contradictions without at the same time offering a concrete alternative or solution for the predicaments analysed. The latter has become the sole criterion according to which every criticism is judged. Think of the reception of the work of documentary activist Michael Moore, especially his *Fahrenheit 9/11* (2004), which investigates the murky reality behind the United States' war against terror both abroad and at home. Even within enlightened circles, it is common to downplay Moore as someone who is always the first to know what is wrong with something and to blame it on someone without ever coming up with a suggestion as to how things could be done better. In the case of *Fahrenheit 9/11*, for example, critics might wonder how Moore *himself* would deal with the undeniably real threat of global terrorism. This allows one to dismiss his critical documentaries as suffering from the same disease inflicted upon the Democrats in the United States who, although extremely critical of Bush, are said to be equally incapable of offering an alternative to war.

This demand for giving concrete alternatives is, of course, the standard way in which people affirm their authority with regard to a certain matter, neutralize any criticism and continue business as usual. Nothing is more effective to silence one's fiercest critics than to simply turn the tables and ask the latter: 'so, since you always seem to know better, what would you do then?' This change of register – from a discussion of problems to one of solutions, from political critique to pragmatic politics – is meant to catch the critic off guard, who as a rule cannot do more than regurgitate the same critical points or mumble some general propositions. The latter is then used to expose the critic as a cowardly, impotent figure deriving some sort of hysterical satisfaction from asking critical questions for the sake of asking them, yet shrugging away from the much more difficult and risky task of assuming responsibility and coming up with concrete solutions to the problems addressed. One can think here of the stream of mocking images of Michael Moore on the internet, in which he is depicted as an overweight, burger-eating, loud-mouthed, irresponsible, decadent, marginal character, manipulative of the facts so as to be able to criticize those in power, thriving on the negative attention he receives, sympathizing with America's enemies, and so on. This is the price to pay for taking one's democratic duty of criticizing too seriously: one is ridiculed as a sick, quarrelsome, pathological figure. The underlying blackmail is thus all too clear: 'either you offer constructive criticism with concrete solutions to go with it or you shut up!'.

It is therefore clear that the demand for constructive criticism deals a direct blow to any real critique. After all, radical critique – by its very nature – cannot immediately be made productive within the existing order since the latter is radically put into question. Radical critique challenges the very standard which measures productivity. It is no coincidence that such censorship – which the demand for concrete counterproposals undoubtedly is – is most often exercised when the critic hits a central nerve of the system, a fundamental issue that cannot be solved without a radical change of the existing order. Precisely the latter makes it so difficult for the critic to respond to this demand, since it asks of him / her the superhuman task of not only creating, through his / her critical labour, a mental space where a radically new set of ideological coordinates could be invented, but also to fill in that space and translate it into practicable policy for everyday situations.

A first, appropriate response on the part of critical forces would be to simply snub this impossible demand and tell those in power to solve their own problems, since *they* created them in the first place and have the mandate and power to do so. In other words, the critic should expose the demand to propose concrete alternatives as illegitimate, unfair and ultimately a sign of the ruling order's *own* impotence. After all, the existing order demands of its critic everything that it (the existing order) – with all its means and expertise – fails to do. By exposing the inappropriateness of this demand, the critic should therefore be able to project his/her alleged impotence back onto the ruling order. The latter, however, is only possible when critical actors stop playing today's game of pragmatic post-politics and defend their right to criticize without offering any alternatives.

### An Executive with an Activist Face

A key scene in the critical documentary *The Corporation* allows us to understand the new norm of constructive criticism as part of a more general mutation, which has become increasingly more prevalent over the past decades – a change in the way in which the ruling order mobilizes society. See documentary The Corporation (Big Picture Media Corporation, 2004), directed by Mark Achbar and Jennifer Abbott. In this scene, we follow a group of other-globalist activists as they organize a sit-in in the backyard of former chairman of Royal Dutch Shell, Sir Mark Moody-Stuart in order to protest against the malpractices of multinational oil companies. To their utmost surprise, the chairman revealed himself as a passionate critic of the oil industry, displaying a clear insight into the many inconvenient truths behind this notoriously dirty industry. Moreover, he claimed that they were not telling him anything *he had not already thought of himself* and that he therefore did not need activists for that. The real question, he retorted, is what they were going to *do* about it. In this way, Moody-Stuart put the ball back in the activists' court while at the same time making himself *an indispensable link in the chain* by making them aware of the fact that although they might not have the power to change anything, he did!

Here we encounter today's ruling order at its most cunning. The shrewd tactics of the former chairman of Shell consists in not only being more critical than the activists but also in accusing them of shrugging away in the face of the enormous challenges ahead: 'if you really think things are so bad, then stop complaining and put your money where your mouth is!' In short, every criticism is interpreted as an unconscious wish for constructive cooperation and, consequently, every critic is treated as a possible ally in finding solutions to remedy the cracks in the system. Even if the activist in question might be in denial about it – so the chairman would undoubtedly argue – what he really wants is a share of power, in order to be able to make a difference.

It was psychoanalyst Jacques Lacan who already in the late sixties theorized this new style of power. Contrary to the classical, authoritarian way of ruling, i.e. by brutally forcing one's own project down society's proverbial throat through sheer use of force and clever manoeuvring, Lacan noticed how the new authority figure – which he called 'the capitalist master' – assumed the same subject position as that of the hysteric. In Lacanian terminology, this subjectivity is symbolized by the letter $, which represents the split subject, the inherent hysterical character of subjectivity, the fact that the core of the subject is a question mark and not some stable, self-certain substance. Lacan's theories of power were part of his discourse theory, which he developed in his Séminaire XVII: L'Envers de la psychanalyse (Paris: Editions du Seuil, 1991). It was in a lecture he gave around the same time (12 / 5 / 1972) at the University of Milan entitled 'Du discours psychanalytique', that he indicated that what is repressed in the traditional master discourse, i.e. the fact that the master is also just a split subject ($), occupies the position of agency in the new, master discourse – which Lacan calls 'capitalist discourse' – and that the master's project – in Lacanian terms,' the Master-signifier (S1) – is inversely repressed. That is to say, the new master wins over the subject by putting his / her cards on the table, by openly listing all weaknesses and problematic features of his / her project. The advantage of the capitalist master is that by presenting herself as her own worst critic – think of the chairman in the above example – she outwits her opponents by robbing them of their ammunition, thereby disabling the standard critical procedure to tirelessly confront the existing order with everything it has to repress in order to simulate its superiority and flawlessness. The lucidity, modesty, enlightenment even, of the new style of power, on the other hand, creates the illusion that the system is receptive to participatory improvement, that there is still significant manoeuvring space that allows for bottom-up input as well as a willingness on the part of those in power to amenably discuss such suggestions and take them into serious consideration. In other words, it creates an atmosphere of horizontality, the feeling that both ruler and ruled are on an equal footing, engaged in a dialogue, and eager to complement each other's capabilities. Consequently, critical actors are seduced into collaborating amicably with their usual enemies about possible solutions to the many problems at hand.

Although the transparency or horizontality displayed by the capitalist master might be evaluated as a great leap forward, it is of course a sham. Let there be no doubt about it, the capitalist master firmly believes – no less than the traditional master that preceded him – that his own (capitalist) project is the only game in town and will sooner or later create heaven on earth. From the chairman's response, for instance, it is clear that criticism of long-term resource depletion, environmental destruction and social deracination does not, to his mind, put in question multinational corporations *as such*. On the contrary, the latter are cleverly presented as the only possible means of solving the problem – lacking only in a more efficient, all-inclusive management of its activities. In short, the difference between the capitalist master and the old authoritarian master is that the former – conscious of the hyper-sensitivity of society to authority issues after centuries of emancipation struggles – *strategically* represses this belief in his own project by fostering an open, interactive approach to society. Note that the capitalist discourse inverts the traditional procedure of interpellation – as formulated by Louis Althusser. It is no longer a case of a figure of authority – a policeman, for instance – shouting 'Hey, you!', and the subject somehow feeling addressed by this call. Capitalist-style interpellation rather works like the figures in Kafka's courts – it pretends not to want anything from you, not to feel too strongly about its own case, even openly doubting and mocking it. The trick here is that it puts the ball in the subject's court. By erasing or confusing its own desire, the capitalist master ensures that the initiative has to come from the subject ('Do you really want to join us? It is up to you!') The capitalist master, in other words, never directly interpellates the subject by convincing the latter of his project, but only indirectly intrigues him/her via a complex dialectic of affirmation and mockery of that project. This sophisticated, virtual style of interpellation, of course, makes it more effective – like a poison slowly seeping into the mind.

Artists Without Borders

It is crucial to see how this new division of labour is more than mere wishful thinking on the side of power, and is increasingly internalized by artists themselves. Faced with an open invitation extended by the same powerful players they used to criticize, artists have reconceptualized their role as socially engaged actors. More precisely, under the motto 'you the power, we the critico-creative thinking', it has led to a more pragmatic interpretation of their critical role and idealism. Most symptomatic in this regard, is the rise, over the past decade, of what might be called 'NGO art' or even – analogous to the humanitarian organization, Doctors Without Borders: 'Art Without Borders'. With such humanitarian organizations, these art practices share the idea that, considering the many urgent needs at hand, there is no call for high art statements, big political manifestoes or sublime expressions of moral indignation. Instead what are needed are direct, concrete, artistic interventions that help disadvantaged populations and communities to deal with the problems they are facing. The latter is seen as the only way in which art can regain its credibility and legitimacy as an engaged force in society, especially after its disastrous 'affair' with modernist, totalitarian ideologies and its more recent surrender to postmodern irony and relativism.

One of the rising stars in this genre is the Dutch artist Jeanne van Heeswijk. Her position more and more resembles that of a conflict consultant, using art as a way to intervene and mediate in heated social situations. Her artistic actions include setting up a temporary museum for contemporary art in abandoned shops in a problem neighbourhood during the time of its restructuring; allowing children to design their own park facilities in the midst of a large-scale urban renewal project; helping residents faced with the destruction of their neighbourhood to construct a collective memory; and running an empty house in a newly built area to accommodate unregulated social practices. It respectively concerns the following projects: De Strip (Vlaardingen, 2002-2004), Face your world, Urban lab (Amsterdam-Slotervaart, 2005), Will o' the Wisp (Rotterdam-Nieuw Crooswijk, 2004-2005), Het blauwe huis (Amsterdam-IJburg, 2005-present). Van Heeswijk is one of a growing army of artists who are travelling around the globe making their artistic-creative skills available for problem assessment and solving – sometimes even anticipating problems or creating problems to dynamize social processes. Whether it concerns the development of a cheap, sustainable and easy way for illegal communities on the border between the United States and Mexico to build their own housing (Estudio Teddy Cruz) or running a popular theatre in a third world slum (26'10 SOUTH Architects), all these projects betray a concern for social empowerment, for small, modest interventions that attempt to improve life in specific situations from the bottom up, in close interaction and participation with local actors and stakeholders. In all these cases, art is redefined in terms of creative consultancy – the act of consulting presented as artwork.

It is clear that in the case of Art Without Borders, the old existentialist motto of the engaged artist of getting one's hands dirty, no longer refers to the tragic compromises and suicidal sacrifices an artist has to make in his/her engagement with a critical or revolutionary project. On the contrary, commitment is understood as the constant production of innovative micro-solutions – so-called 'pocket revolutions' – to the real, everyday problems people encounter in their immediate life world. This constitutes a fundamental move away from any deep criticism, away from a critical art practice that throws fundamental questions at the ruling order and tirelessly confronts it with its inconvenient truths, towards an art practice devoted to providing answers, solutions, toolkits and DIY-manuals for the problems at hand, often in close cooperation with market players or public instances.

Over the last decade, this 'Art Without Borders' has developed into an alternative art scene outside the official circuit of museums and art institutions, receiving considerable budgets and funding. However, this NGO art can be seen as the worldly counterpart of a contemporary movement within contemporary museum art proper. We are thinking here of the so-called relational art, as theorized by Nicolas Bourriaud, which is also explicitly positioned against the critical art tradition – that, for example, in the sixties ceaselessly confronted society with its contradictions so as to dialectically supersede the existing order and revolutionize society down to its every fibre. Relational art, on the contrary, aims at experimenting with new social relations in micro-situations such as a happening in a gallery space, for example. Instead of provoking the audience into action through confrontation with the violence and injustice of the current order, relational art is all about generating positive experiences in small, controlled settings, which might then form the basis of a renewal of social relations at large. For a critique of this relational art practice, see BAVO, 'Let Art Save Democracy! Or: Can Relational Art Also Subvert Today's Imperative to Re-stage Non-capitalist Social Relations in this so-called Post-utopian Age?', in: Metahaven, Regimes of Representation. Art & Politics beyond the House of the People, conference proceedings volume (2006). This pragmatic turn is experienced by the proponents of NGO art as a sort of home-coming. After art's disastrous adventure with politics in the twentieth century, it is now returning to what it can do best: to engage with the world in a no-nonsense way and, through experiment and play, offer creative solutions for real problems. The cultural agent is, in short, recast as a homo pragmaticus who – averse to and free from any political agenda or ideological distortions – engages with society.

However noble the intentions of this Art Without Borders might be, or perhaps precisely because of its noble intentions, it is a valued ally of the current system that, as sociologist Pierre Bourdieu rightly puts it, is more and more evolving into a two-pronged system of hard, economic sectors as its right hand, and soft, social sectors as its left hand. The right hand is mercilessly cutting jobs in the name of efficiency and imposing market norms on every human activity – leaving a social wasteland in its wake. The left hand – the soft, social sectors – is then asked to patch things up within ever stricter budgetary confines. See Pierre Bourdieu, Acts of Resistance. Against the New Myths of Our Time (Cambridge: Polity Press, 1998). Because of their inborn empathy for the underdog, their willingness to work pro deo and their ability to win the hearts and minds of the people, artists are increasingly enlisted in the left-hand side of this schizophrenic system. In this way, the art sector is reduced to cannon fodder for a system in which socio-cultural programmes are increasingly becoming not only merely palliative – i.e. limited to damage control – but also purely symbolic, i.e. meant to give the victims left behind in neo-liberalism's incessant march forward the feeling that they are not just left by the wayside but still somehow count.

The crucial question is whether NGO artists, with their micro-interventions, also *politicize* the larger injustices and skewed power relations that are at play in the context in which they operate. In other words, do they also problematize the mechanisms responsible for producing today's 'homo sucker' – as Slavoj Žižek calls the many victims of the current world order? Slavoj Žižek, Welcome to the Desert of the Real: Five Essays on September 11 and Related Dates (London: Verso, 2002) 71. It is here that Art Without Borders more often than not falls short. In the heated social and political situations in which they work – one can say that they deal with the reverse side of capitalism's magical recovery from its near-death experience in the mid-seventies – their highly specific and practical interventions cannot but strike one as too modest, naive, somewhat childish and misplaced, especially in light of the violent, systemic nature of the deeper causes behind the local problems addressed. In the case of Jeanne van Heeswijk's interventions within major restructuring schemes of neighbourhoods for instance, the underlying neo-liberal and neo-conservative mechanisms are never problematized as such or tackled with the same vigour and creative energy and attention that is devoted to the emotional and mental health of the victims of the restructuring. Still, it is neo-liberal kill or cure measures that are responsible for the victimization of these population groups and their condemnation to an uncertain future. For this critique, see BAVO, 'Neoliberalism with Dutch Characteristics. The Big Fix-up of the Netherlands and the Practice of Embedded Cultural Activism', in: Maria Hlavajova (et al.), Citizens and Subjects. The Netherlands, for example (Zürich: JRP-Ringier, 2007) 51-63.

One of the reasons why Art Without Borders fails to confront systemic issues in their interventions, is no doubt their adherence to a pragmatico-humanitarian ideology, with its emphasis on inventing concrete solutions that can be directly implemented – which is of course a manifestation of today's norm of constructive critique. The urge of NGO artists for concrete actions *a priori* limits the scope for action and shuts off the possibility of a radical questioning of the existing order, since the latter is needed – or at least, so it is assumed – for the realization of those actions. In other words, their addiction to doing something useful in the face of the needy other – which is elevated into some Levinasian Other – makes them *dependent* for the implementation of their initiatives on the same order that produced those needy in *the first place*. For this reason, artists have to repress the more fundamental problems at play in the context of the work. NGO art thus succumbs to what one might call the humanitarian fallacy, the idea that before one gets on one's high horse and aims at changing the world in its entirety, one first has to offer relief to the victims, the motto of the humanitarian mind being: 'victims first, politics later'. In practice, however, this often implies: 'No politics please, victims only'. The humanitarian's reasoning is that taking an explicit political stance would endanger care for the victims, since it might cause opposition from the same authorities that are needed to deliver the goods in the field. This denial of politics leads to an excessive focus on the 'what' – i.e. on what can be done, how it is to be done, etc. – that overshadows the 'that' – i.e. outrage over the fact that there is something fundamentally wrong, the political causes, etc. We can say that the obsession of the engaged artist to immediately think in terms of practicable solutions leads to a pragmatic blinding, that is, today's variety of the ideological blinding so heavily criticized after the proclamation of the end of ideology. If ideological blinding referred to the denial or distortion of reality caused by an allegiance to an abstract set of beliefs and values that overdetermines the interpretation of reality and censors out all incompatible elements, and thereby seriously limits the scope for practical action, pragmatic blinding inversely means the censoring of a certain conceptualization of reality based on its alleged unproductivity for practice. We can thus also speak of a censorship from practice.

The paradox – or tragedy even – of Art Without Borders is the fact that precisely the eagerness of cultural agents to immediately get down to business and make a difference prevents them from acting in a way that would be appropriate to the bigger stakes of the context, as this immediacy sits uneasily with a radical critique of the existing order. This argument is fully developed in our forthcoming book, Too Active to Act. Cultural Activism After the End of History (unpublished manuscript). In practice, NGO art more often than not leads to a diarrhoea of unconnected, highly specific, ad hoc interventions that, although offering instant relief, extinguishes any possibility of a long-term solution.

Always Choose the Worst Option

Faced with such criticism, NGO artists will no doubt resort to the bottom-line argument that their actions at least succeed in making the world a slightly better place; that those most affected by the injustices of the current world order now at least have some means at their disposal to improve their living conditions or to socially empower themselves. We here encounter the true colours of Art Without Borders: it is not aimed at the deposition of the existing order, but rather at 'making the best of a bad situation'. In short, although aware of the many flaws and injustices in today's world, they do not believe they have the power to change or even challenge forces like capitalism or representative democracy. As a result, they rather focus on the small things they *can* change, on doing the best they can under less than perfect circumstances, on making a difference, however minimal, in the here and now. This argument is sometimes also sublimated into a professional ethic, i.e. the fact that it would be unprofessional to interfere in matters that fall outside of one's creative expertise ('who is the artist to say that capitalism is bad?'). The latter is seen as a duty, since a *minimally improved* order is far more preferable than the existing order *as such*. In this sense, it differs greatly from more radical positions, i.e. positions of resistance that start from the premise that there is something so fundamentally wrong with the existing order that every attempt at making it better, however well-intended, will always be perverted by it, and that one should thus aim for nothing less than the radical subversion of that order. In light of this radical position, there is no doubt something self-defeating in the position of NGO artists. They depart from the premise that radical, global change is impossible, and consequently limit themselves to the invention of highly specific solutions designed for local contexts, which makes global change even more unlikely. In short, it is as if they throw in the towel too quickly and shrug away from the much more difficult task of forcing a fundamental change in mindset. NGO art also differs from those forms of resistance that – even though they do not see the possibility of a fundamental change in the near future – do not self-censor their critical potential from the get-go, but at least question the ruling ideological coordinates.

In the remainder of this essay, we will pursue this more radical line of artistic resistance. We will follow Karl Kraus's provocative suggestion that in being forced to choose between two evils, one should always choose the worst evil. This would imply that, as an artist, one would have to give up the will to resist *altogether*; to stop trying – like the pragmatic idealists – to be the 'idealist in the machine', patiently and tirelessly ironing out the rough edges of the system. Instead of fleeing from the suffocating closure of the current system, one is now incited to fully immerse oneself in it, even contributing to the closure. To choose the worst option, in other words, means no longer trying to make the best of the current order, but precisely to *make the worst* of it, to turn it into the worst possible version of itself. It would thus entail a refusal of the current blackmail in which artists are offered all kinds of opportunities to make a difference, on the condition that they give up on their desire for radical change.

We call this strategy that of *over-identification*. This term was coined by Slavoj Žižek to denote the unique subversive strategy of the Slovenian avant-garde group Laibach in communist Yugoslavia of the eighties. See Slavoj Žižek, 'Why are Laibach and NSK not fascists?', in: M'ARS (Ljubljana: Moderna Galerija, 1993), vol. 3/4. See also: Slavoj Žižek, 'On (un-)changing canons and extreme avant-gardes', lecture on the symposium 'East of Art: Transformations in Eastern Europe', MOMA New York, 23/3/2003. Unlike the stereotypical Eastern European dissident movement – whose model is no doubt the Polish Solidarność movement – pleading for a humanization and relaxation of the communist regimes, Laibach challenged the communist regime by accusing them of being too lax, too soft, lacking belief in their own system. Inversely, Laibach's performances, in which a powerful potion of Stalinist and Nazi symbols was dished up, strategically pleaded for an ultra-orthodox communism that was *even more tough* than its 'real-life' counterpart. In this way, they succeeded in embarrassing the communist rulers that felt out-flanked on all sides, both left and right. It is this strategy of choosing the worst option – in this case between a communism with a human face and an even tougher, thoroughly inhuman communism – that we shall explore in the following section, applying it to today's *topoi* of resistance. We can here briefly mention two other strategies of artistic resistance of the radical type that are propagated today. The first is the strategy of doing nothing, the idea that artists should withdraw themselves from a system that thrives on the idealism of artists, that uses the latter's freshness to constantly revolutionize itself, thereby pulling the plug on that system. This strategy is today's variety of what, in the high days of May '68, was called 'marginalism': young people preferring life in the margins of society above participation in the regular economy. The problem with this strategy is that this marginality is internalized and accommodated within today's order, think of the way our oil-companies invent relaxed regimes for activists within the company structure. The second often propagated strategy is that of inventing new deep ideals, a new vision of society, that can feed/motivate a wide countermovement, so as to move outside or beyond of the existing ideological co-ordinates of capitalism or representative democracy. Problematic in this case, is where artists could find inspiration – if it is not to be some creation ex nihilo – for such alternative vision in the present system, that more and more closes in on itself and its subjects, and limits, controls even, their mental horizon? In other words, how radically new can such a vision be, so as to be able to resist the notorious capacity of capitalism to feed off other value systems?

Giving a Big 'Yes' to Capitalism

It is precisely such over-identification with the enemy that is applied in the documentary *The Yes Men*, the story of activists Mike Bonanno and Andy Bichlbaum – who call themselves 'the Yes Men' – posing as representatives of the World Trade Organization (WTO), one of the key neo-liberal global financial institutions. In the bogus lectures they present ever so seriously at conferences and at universities, their strategy is to present the official discourse of the WTO in its pure, unmediated form, that is, stripped of any form of sugar-coating such as ethical sensibilities, concern for poverty or respect for democracy. Recall, for example, the hilarious scene in which one of the Yes Men participates as a representative of the WTO in a television debate on global injustice and the role of financial institutions. The usual trick of genuine representatives on such debates is, of course, to water down their own policies or couch them in euphemistic terms, so as to prevent being attacked by the opponents head-on. The Yes Men, on the contrary, bluntly and openly propagated all kinds of hardcore neo-liberal arguments and schemes, to the obvious confusion of the other participants in the debate. As fake WTO representatives, they emphasized, for example, the WTO's alliance with big corporate power structures, presenting it as something natural. They even insisted that the works of neo-liberal thinkers such as Milton Friedman should be obligatory reading for school children. This open confession of an absolutely anti-democratic policy totally flabbergasted his main opponent in the debate, a wide-eyed otherglobalist barely able to utter the words: 'well, that's clear then'.

However, the real target of the Yes Men's performance is the WTO itself, which finds itself in an awkward position. The latter is faced not with a sceptic laying bare the inconvenient truths behind its policies – which can easily be denied or given a spin – but rather with someone who over-enthusiastically identifies with their position, completely annihilating any critical distance and fully endorsing the WTO pro-gramme and ideology. Confronted with such display of ultra-orthodox neo-liberalism, the WTO cannot but tone down its own message and emphasize how neo-liberalism should not be taken as the only game in town. After all, it cannot possibly solve all of the world's problems by itself. In other words, the Yes Men's strategy of over-identification forces their opponent, the WTO, to betray the articles of its faith, to deny its passionate attachment to the neo-liberal programme and admit defeat, which makes it – instead of its critics – appear weak.

The critical effectiveness of the Yes Men consists in being too honest and sympathetic towards the WTO, thereby they succeed in bringing into the open the 'neo-liberal utopia of unlimited exploitation' – as Bourdieu phrased it. See Pierre Bourdieu, Acts of resistance. Against the new myths of our time (Cambridge: Polity Press, 1998). Think of the entertaining scene in which the two Yes Men posed as WTO representatives at a student conference. There they proposed a scheme to solve the world's hunger problem by reprocessing the faeces of McDonald's customers into hamburgers for the Third World – thereby cashing in on its leftover nutritional value. What should be the ultimate wet dream of any neo-liberal adherent – not having to apologize for what s/he wants, being able to openly exploit a profitable opportunity while at the same time concocting a profitable solution for the third world's food shortage – somehow fails to result in a utopian world in which the freedom and dignity of all is secured. Instead, it leads to a frightening, immoral universe of cold and ruthless calculation. The Yes Men, in other words, rush in where neo-liberals fear to tread by applying neo-liberal *doxa* more consistently, rigorously and ruthlessly – thus beating them at their own game and laying bearing the ugly dystopian kernel of the neo-liberal utopia.

Such explicit, uncut rendering of the ultimate consequences of a social formation, makes the strategy of over-identification an effective antidote against what cultural philosopher Peter Sloterdijk describes as today's all-pervasive cynicism, in which people know very well that there is something fundamentally wrong with something, yet continue to act as if they don't. See Peter Sloterdijk, Kritik der zynischen Vernunft (Frankfurt am Main: Suhrkamp, 1983). Recall how, in one of the Yes Men's fake WTO presentations, the public – a gathering of highly educated people – uncritically endures the scandalous proposals of abject nonsense staged by the two activists or, at least, gives them the benefit of the doubt. As we argued earlier, this doubt is actively maintained by the capitalist discourse by presenting itself as an open system conscious of its own problems and ready to take into account critical suggestions or consider alternatives. This attitude causes people to let go of their criticism and to conveniently repress their knowledge about the terrible backside of our capitalist society, assuming that the latter cannot possibly be that perverted, immoral or unjust. This tendency to always think the best of something, to believe that 'things can't possibly be that fundamentally screwed up', is the stuff ideology is made from. Ideology always parasitizes on the urge of people to believe the unbelievable, to make sense of the meaningless, to make plausible the implausible, since the reality of living in an inconsistent, meaningless world is, at least for the majority of people, experienced as unbearable. Consequently, faced by an inconsistent, unjust social system, people try to make it consistent at all costs – almost as if their life depended on it, which, in a way, it does. So, all the current order has to do, is to encourage such a sympathetic reading by the subject, to provide the footage, the materials to produce reasonable doubt in the subject. In this sense, one can say that the subject does the difficult job for this order, proving its case, legitimizing it, tying the loose ends together.

This cynical subjective mode is, of course, only possible because we are never truly confronted with what we are doing, with the consequences of our capitalist lifestyle. Along with revealing documentaries exposing all kinds of inconvenient truths, today's subject is also bombarded by arguments that keep his/her disgust or shame in check – well below the level at which people start demanding instant and radical change. Even supposed critics of global financial institutions such as the WTO, like macroeconomist Joseph Stiglitz, argue that if economic globalization were to be managed better, the high profits of corporations will eventually trickle down to the world's poorest population. In short, after having sat through the onslaught of nightmarish scenes of global destitution that come pouring into our living rooms every evening, we can rest assured and continue to participate with a clear conscience in the same system that produces that destitution.

The strategy of over-identification owes its effectiveness to the fact that it sabotages this dialectic of alarm and reassurance, fear and relief, by ruthlessly dishing up the system in its most extreme form – a side that the system itself strategically conceals. This strategy clearly proved to be highly effective in the Yes Men's presentation of the faeces-recycling scheme, mentioned above. The latter provoked disbelief in the audience, even anger, with people walking out fuming. It clearly pushed people who might otherwise have a more nuanced or relativist attitude towards the current state of affairs, to the point where they cannot bare it any longer and feel compelled to take a radical stance. The act of over-identification, in other words, eliminates the subject's reflex to make excuses for the current order and to invent ways to 'manage it better' so as to overcome or at least smooth over the problems. The strategy of over-identification could thus not be more opposed to Gilles Deleuze's 'alcoholic' ethics of always stopping before the last glass, so as to be able to sustain one's desire for liquor. This is, of course, also the trick of the capitalist master who is careful not to overpower or 'drown' it subjects with its ideology, offering it in small doses instead. Over-identification, on the other hand, as the Yes Men's performances illustrate, is closer to Søren Kierkegaard's 'emetic', which entails deliberately swallowing too much of the loved poison – overdoing it – so as to be able to break with it for good, to cut the ties with the ambivalent love object.

Producing the Contradiction

The action *Bitte liebt Österreich!* of theatremaker Christoph Schlingensief in Vienna in 2000, allows us to further sharpen our analysis of the concept of over-identification. *The event was part of the Wiener Festwoche and took place from 6 – 11 June. See Matthias Lilienthal and Claus Philipp, Schlingensiefs Ausländer Raus (Frankfurt am Main: Suhrkamp, 2000); as well as Paul Poet's documentary, Ausländer Raus. Schlingensief's container (Monitorpop entertainment, 2005).* Schlingensief's intervention was meant as a protest against the extreme right party of Jörg Haider (FPÖ) joining the Austrian government. In an improvised container camp, he organized a *Big Brother* show in which asylum seekers had to curry favour with the Austrian people, in order not to be voted off the show and out of the country. The banner on top of the container camp stated the latter in no uncertain terms: *Ausländer raus!* The fact that this event took place in the heart of Austria's capital, right in front of the Burgtheater, gave it a high visibility both nationally and internationally, with crowds assembling daily in front of the camp.

As should be clear from the ultra-racist content of the banner, as well as the sadistic concept of the *Big Brother* show, Schlingensief over-identifies with the populist-right discourse. By overstating the latter, he tries to *visualize* the violence of the new Right, which is, of course, rarely ever expressed as such by its proponents. While racist slogans such as 'foreigners out!' are commonly used in rallies to mobilize people – often by party members low in the party hierarchy – in official discourse these slogans are couched in euphemistic terms or given a democratic twist. We can thus say that one finds the capitalist discourse where one least expects it. Even today's proponents of extreme right thinking – what philosopher Etienne Balibar calls 'neo-racism' – present themselves as self-reflective and enlightened – no longer clinging to some biogenetic race theory, but merely affirming the naturalness or inevitability of cultural differences. See Etienne Balibar and Immanuel Wallerstein, Race, Nation, Class. Ambiguous Identities (London: Verso, 1991). For the often hilarious manifestations of such neo-racism, one can think of the 2005 campaign of the Flemish extreme right political party Vlaams Belang (Flemish Interest) in Morocco, in which some party members went to have talks with Moroccan politicians, stating what a wonderful country Morocco was, praising the country for the friendliness of its people, its rich culture, good business climate, and, inversely, making negative promotion of their own country, accentuating its notoriously dreary climate, slacking economy and individualist lifestyle. The hidden message behind this song of praise to the Other is of course that the latter should return to, or stay in his own country. It is the distorted, 'positivized' form of the classic racist argument against foreigners who complain about their poor life circumstances: 'if you really are unhappy here, why don't you go back to your own country!' By presenting his show as a FPÖ event, Schlingensief cut through this political correct facade, exaggerating precisely those racist statements that are diluted or distorted in official Right-wing discourse. Think also of his tactics not to argue with his critics or convince them of their wrong, but to simply repeat their arguments, slogans and insults through his megaphone, the amplification of which exposes the hollowness of their arguments even more, as well as the violence that drives them – the latter of course to the further agony of the opponents. It was Walter Benjamin who apropos the work of Karl Kraus remarked how more effective than critically commenting on something, is to simply quote what you're criticizing.

However, Schlingensief's strategy cannot entirely be reduced to one of over-identification or, to be more precise, the latter is constantly contradicted by his insults and provocations levelled against the new Right. Take the banner, for example, which functions both as an over-affirmation of the right-wing imaginary and as a challenge to the right-wing government, since Schlingensief repeatedly mocks the stupidity of this government for allowing such an utterly racist banner to hang in front of the Opera House for the whole world to see. He also encourages tourists to take pictures of his event and to spread the word at home that 'this is Austria', that the latter has turned into a fascist regime. This constant shifting between opposing positions – between over-statement, on the one hand, and mockery or critique, on the other – is an express attempt by Schlingensief to produce the contradiction, which is how he defines the task of artistic resistance. See Paul Poet, Ausländer Raus. Schlingensief's container (Monitorpop entertainment, 2005). In this documentary, Schlingensief also describes his modus operandi as: 'inviting a multitude of systems to gather in a dance and that dance becomes the picture'. Or, as one commentator put it, Schlingensief creates situations that not only are not clear, but also *cannot* be made clear.

This deliberate *structural ambiguity* makes Schlingensief's *Big Brother* show the exact opposite of the performances of the Yes Men discussed earlier, as the latter strive towards a sort of hyper-clarity of position: 'I am a hardcore neo-liberal, let there be no doubt about that'. The Yes Men aim to present the enemy in the clearest way possible, fully endorsing the discourse of the opponent, perhaps only revealing a critical stance in the extreme clarity that is strived for. One way of explaining this difference is to say that the aim of both the Yes Men and Schlingensief is to confuse, but that they use different tactics to do so. The former's tactic entails an exaggerated over-identification with something that invariably provokes disbelief that anybody can believe that uncritically in something. The latter, on the other hand, confuses by osculating between over-identification and critique, by giving out mixed, highly contradictory signals, thereby depriving the audience of any stable vantage point from which to cognitively map the event.

The advantage of Schlingensief's version of over-identification is no doubt that it sabotages an easy interpretation of, or identification with the intervention, which makes it more difficult for both enemies and allies to discard or recuperate it. This became very clear when anti-fascist activists stormed the container camp to liberate the asylum seekers, violently tearing down the banner in the process. It revealed how the oscillation between over-identification and critique of *Bitte liebt Österreich!*, produces an uneasy situation for both the Right and Left: while the former cannot simply discard Schlingensief's action as a platform for Leftist propaganda because of its use of Rightwing power-language, the latter cannot simply label it as fascist either due to the simultaneous critical comments on the FPÖ. *This undecidability with regards to its position is also what Slavoj Žižek pinpoints as the strength of the strategy of over-identification. As he writes about Laibach and their in-breeding of Stalinist and Nazi symbols: 'By means of the elusive character of their desire, the indecidability as to "where they actually stand", Laibach compels us to take up our position and decide upon our desire.' (See Slavoj Žižek, 'Why are Laibach and NSK not fascists?', in: M'ARS (Ljubljana: Moderna Galerija, 1993), vol. 3/4.)* Also, neither of the two camps can intervene in Schlingensief's event without reproducing their own, internal contradictions. This is most obvious for the Right: removing the ultra-racist banner actually contradicts what they really want, i.e. a tough asylum policy – thereby running the risk of alienating the rank and file. However, as the violent attack of the anti-racist movement demonstrated, Schlingensief's *Big Brother* also confronted the extreme left with the inconsistency of its position. Their attack revealed that, while hyperactive in organizing all kinds of protest rallies, they are not willing to liberate the real camps for asylum seekers with the same bravery and destructive zeal as they did Schlingensief's staged version. Further, as Schlingensief remarked mockingly, just how free could the unfortunate participants in Austria be, where an entire system is in place to remove them as quickly and efficiently as possible from the Austrian territory. One could therefore say that, instead of being liberated, they will merely exchange their fictitious prison in the *Big Brother* house for a real one. In short, given the fact that reality is much more cynical than Schlingensief's staging of it, we can understand Schlingensief sneering at the activists, calling them 'a self-deceiving demonstration culture'. *See Paul Poet, Ausländer Raus. Schlingensief's container (Monitorpop entertainment, 2005).*

Perhaps we can say that the Yes Men, in the extremity with which they apply the concept of over-identification, are clearly *activists* – the radical, uncritical character of their identification with neo-liberalism being the opposite manifestation of their radical denouncement of it, i.e. their sympathy for the otherglobalist movement. As a result, once one realizes that they are fraudsters, both camps can easily give them a place: the WTO can dismiss them as impostors, while the otherglobalists can welcome them as sympathizers to their cause. Due to its deliberate impurity, Schlingensief's *Bitte liebt Österreich!* resists any such easy recuperation and goes further than the Yes Men by allowing neither their friends nor their foes to sit back self-complacently and relax.

Conclusion: No More Mister Nice Guy

To the question of artistic resistance, the *topos* of over-identification thus provides an uneasy answer. It demands of cultural producers to stop being Mister Nice Guy and to sacrifice their ingrained urge

to counter societal cynicism with an offensive of idealism. The latter –
so much should be clear by now – turns them into easy victims for
the capitalist masters of this world. The strategy of over-identification
is precisely aimed against this idealist reflex to do the right thing.
Think, for example, of Schlingensief's comment regarding
his *Big Brother* show: 'it's not an Amnesty International Project, it's
not a "show me your wounds" project, it is a *Schweinische Unternehmung*'
– a swinish enterprise! Or, what to think of the action of Dutch
artist Martijn Engelbregt who distributed fake, pseudo-governmental
inquiries in Amsterdam in which people were asked to communicate
all kinds of information with regards to supposed illegal residents living
in their area. Martijn Engelbregt operates under the name of EGBG,
which stands for 'Engelbregt Gegevens Beheer Groep' (which could
be translated as Engelbregt Data Administration Agency). The action took
place under the cover name of Regoned, which is short for Registratie Orgaan Nederland (Registrational Body
of the Netherlands). About 200,000 forms were distributed at the end of December 2003. This action
immediately caused a wave of outrage and protest. It not only triggered
bad associations with the Nazi occupation during the Second World
War and the deportation of many Jews – in which the local government
and population played a dubious role – it also focalized discontent
about the recent hardening of Dutch immigration law. The artist came
under heavy attack from all sides – within art circles he was criticized
for his unethical behaviour, his dangerous manipulation of people's
deep-seated feelings. This was the price to pay for radicalizing
people's attitude towards policies they otherwise silently endure. One can
see Engelbregt's action as the reversal of the civil disobedience of several mayors of Dutch cities to deport residing
asylum seekers, which led to all kinds of emotional confessions on national media of mayors who 'as a person'
could not do this to 'another human being'. The latter, however, had the paradoxical effect of only adding to the
popularity of the then Minister for Immigration and Integration Rita Verdonk – notorious for her Right-wing,
zero-tolerance attitudes – who got elected to most popular politician in the same year. Against the disobedience
of the mayors, Engelbregt, with his action, on the contrary, resisted the system by what one could call a
civil over-obedience, the advantage of which is that it now forces the existing order in a defensive, weak position,
since the latter now have to explain how they would never go that far, etc.

It is clear that by enthusiastically joining ranks with
the enemy, the artist invariably also strikes
a blow at him/herself or, at least, at the
Other in him/herself, the internalized myth of the artist as the
last idealist, the one who, with his experi-
mental attitude, is the ideal troubleshooter in
a system plagued by internal problems and conflicts. It was such
'symbolic suicide' – the self-sacrifice of the idealist within the artist –
that was staged by artist Christoph Büchel at *Manifesta* 4 in 2002.

He sold his exhibition slot on E-Bay to the highest bidder and so cashed in early on the surplus value added to his symbolic capital by his selection for this international art fair. Christoph Büchel's action was entitled Invite yourself. It is obvious that the artist intentionally provokes society with the subversive question why he – and art in general – should be an exception when it comes to manipulating the laws of supply and demand for self-enrichment. Or, put differently, why art cannot be as ruthlessly self-interested or nakedly capitalist as everybody else?

By such radical refusal of the role transferred to art of protecting society from what it wants, the art of over-identification creates a suffocating closure within the system, no longer allowing its subjects any escape from its immanent laws. In this way, society can no longer delegate its task to resist the obvious injustices of today's order to the safe haven of art but is forced to face this task of subversion itself.

Appendix: the Unbearable Lightness of Hyper-Idealism

We are compelled to add one last complication to our analysis of the strategy of over-identification, which hinges on the question what exactly one over-identifies with. In what preceded, we focused on artistic actions that over-identify with the worst side of the existing order, i.e. its neo-capitalist, neo-racist, neo-conservative programme. There is, however, also the opposite possibility: to over-identify with ideals such as freedom or human rights, which the existing order has to evoke in order to implement its programme and to convince society of its superiority.

This, what one could call, positive over-identification is extremely relevant in an age in which the dialectic between the Law and its obscene underside – as thematized by Slavoj Žižek, for example – is radically reversed by the capitalist discourse. See Slavoj Žižek, Plague of Phantasies (London: Verso, 1997). In its classical form, this dialectic describes the fact that every system has to maintain a distance from the very ideals it propagates. As a result, it is always split into an official level – 'the letter of the law' – and an unwritten universe of jokes, cynicism and mockery of those official ideals – 'the obscene underside of the law'. The latter is, of course, repressed, it can never see the light of day or be acknowledged as such – in undistorted form – at the official level. Today, on the contrary, in the capitalist discourse it is the official ideals that are repressed, since the slightest hint of any residual belief in some Grand Narrative or absolute truth is enough to be disqualified, to be treated like a pariah. Truth has, in other words, become an obscene, dirty little secret, something confined to the private sphere that is relativized and mocked in real life. Inversely, it is the obscene underside that has become the official norm, brought home by the fact that we are continuously being commanded to deconstruct all deep beliefs and mock our passionate attachments.

This reversal of the traditional dialectic makes it subversive once more to over-identify with the system's repressed ideals. It would amount to what Jacques Rancière, calls 'confirming the appearance, i.e. instead of criticizing the system's alleged ideals for their merely formal character and their betrayal in practice, it takes them dead seriously and demands their uncompromised application in real life. Jacques Rancière, La Mésentente. Politique et philosophie (Paris: Galilée, 1995) 126.

He gives the example of the French labour movement in the nineteenth century who used the system's lip-service to the declaration of the universal rights of men as a leverage to obtain the right to vote for normal workers.

We can find a lot of examples of this strategy in the documentaries of Michael Moore. One might even say that he is at his most subversive when he usurps the ideals of his opponents – that of freedom and democracy – as opposed to revealing the dirty facts behind their policies. Think, for instance, of the scene in *Fahrenheit 9/11* in which Moore plays the devil's advocate by harassing members of congress who voted in favour of the war in Iraq, by asking them to send their sons and daughters to Iraq, so as to set a good example of what it means to sacrifice what one holds dearest for the sake of freedom. Moore's enthusiasm caused the congressmen, all of whom came up with all kinds of petty excuses, to become greatly embarrassed and to reveal their true colours: despite their rhetoric, they certainly never believed the war to be that noble so as to send their own offspring.

We can also think of Moore's soundtrack album of Fahrenheit 9/11, composed of naively affirmative songs on America's ideal of freedom. See Songs And Artists That Inspired Fahrenheit 9/11 (Sony, 2004). BAVO, 'The spectre of the Avant-Garde. Contemporary reassertions of the programme of subversion in cultural production', in: Andere Sinema 176 (2006) 38.

In short, Moore strategically identifies with the *utopian* core of American patriotism – i.e. its universal aspiration, the fact that everybody can be an American – to provoke its *betrayal* and *corruption* in everyday politics. Moore makes visible how the practical implementation of the ideals of freedom – the liberation of people all around the globe from evil dictators – is in actual fact used as a cover for securing the interests of multinational companies and the United States at large. Of course, the subversive force of this strategy lies in the exaggerated belief in the ideal – a *hyper*-idealism, which radically represses the common assumption that all ideals are corrupted by reality or cannot be realized except by making compromises. It asks of the artist to play dumb and to insist, like an idiot, on the ruthless application of the ideals to social reality, without granting any exception.

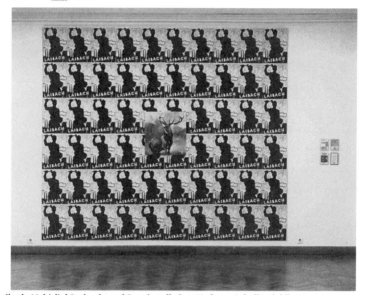

**Laibach, *Multiplied Steelworker and Stag*, installation, Moderna Galerija, Ljubljana (2004)**
A grid of posters representing a socialist steelworker with a painting of a stag superimposed in the middle. *Photo and copyright: Laibach*

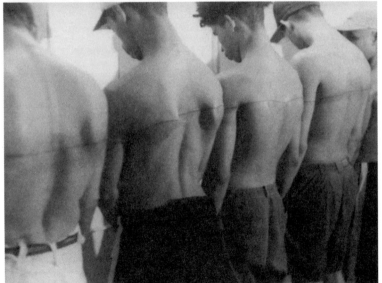

**Santiago Sierra, 250 cm line tattooed on 6 paid people, Espacio Aglutinador, Havana (1999)**
Unemployed Cuban Youngsters having a line tattooed on their backs
in return for $ 30. Copyright: Santiago Sierra and Lisson Gallery, London

**Atelier Van Lieshout, AVL-*Ville*, installation, Rotterdam (2001)**
On an abandoned plot in the port of Rotterdam a free-state was decreed to experiment
with artistic freedom, anarchy and autarky. *Photo and copyright: Atelier Van Lieshout*

**Irwin, *Portrait of the Deer*, mixed media (1986)**
Series of icons in which the symbol of the stag is juxtaposed
with modernist motifs. *Photo and copyright: Irwin*

Christoph Schlingensief, *Bitte liebt Österreich!*, action, Vienna (2002),
still taken from Paul Poet's documentary *Ausländer Raus. Schlingensief's Container* (2005)
*Big Brother* show in which the Austrian people could vote asylum seekers off the
show and out of the country. Copyright: Monitorpop Entertainment

**Michael Moore, *Fahrenheit 9/11*, still taken from the movie (2004)**
Pro-war U.S. congressmen are encouraged to set a good example by sending
their sons and daughters to Iraq. Copyright: Lionsgate Films

# SlaveCity

**Atelier Van Lieshout, *SlaveCity*, mixed media (2005)**
A forced labour camp for 200,000 inmates combining state of the art technological innovation with the latest management skills for maximum profit. *Photo and copyright: Atelier Van Lieshout*

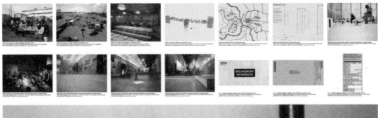

**Jens Haaning, *Superdiscount*, installation, Fri-Art, Fribourg (1998)**
By importing consumer items from France to Switzerland as art objects, visitors
to the gallery could acquire the goods up 35 % cheaper. *Photo and copyright: Jens Haaning*

**Mike Bonanno and Andy Bichlbaum, *The Yes Men*, action, still taken from the movie directed by among others Dan Ollman (2003)** Two anti-corporate activists lecturing on the latest developments in labour disciplining at an economic forum, posing as representatives of the WTO.

# The Myth of the Slovene Stag:
## Neue Slowenische Kunst and the Reprocessing of Traditional Symbolism

by Alexei Monroe

Over-identification is often discussed in terms of ideology, performance or politics. However, the specific visual, sonic and symbolic motifs used to produce over-identification effects sometimes receive less attention. Therefore it may be useful to explore one of the most commonly used motifs of the *Neue Slowenische Kunst* (NSK), the Stag. An understanding of the dynamics associated with this is critical to any detailed analysis of NSK's 'retrograde' mode of over-identification. There are similarities between NSK and the 'symbolic Stag' that appears in folklore, art and mass visual culture. Both have seemingly clear meanings but are actually more transitory and multi-faceted and NSK's 'Slovene Stag' leaves elusive and illusory tracks and scents. In Celtic tradition it is one of the three oldest animals and the emergence of such a primeval symbol in ultra-contemporary underground culture at first seems surprising but this only underlines its continued and surprising relevance within the most unlikely contexts.

Over-identification is a term first associated with the actions of the group Laibach Kunst in early eighties Yugoslavia. Slavoj Žižek later theorized it in his 1993 article, 'Why are Laibach and NSK not Fascists?' See http://nskstate.com/appendix/articles/why_are_laibach.php He described what he called an 'aggressive inconsistent mixture' of contradictory symbolisms that had the effect of 'bringing to light the obscene superego underside of the system' by seeming to over-identify with its rituals. He also stresses that this is linked to the doubt and fear created by these interventions, effects generated by the lack of the usual artistic-ironic distance towards kitsch, propaganda and other elements that tend to alarm so-called 'enlightened intellectuals.' One tactical question that emerges from NSK's work is whether a symbol such as the Stag is irredeemably kitsch or reactionary, or whether its manipulation can produce valuable and unexpected effects.

### Dictation of the Motif

'Our work refers to the entire history of art, politics and mankind in general.' – Laibach See http://www.nskstate.com/laibach/ interviews/excerpts-91-95.php

NSK over-identifies or seems to over-identify with a series of mental, ideological and cultural regimes. It has attracted most attention and condemnation for its use of totalitarian symbolism. However, one means by which it has created the semi-illusory spectacle of a national cultural movement has been the use of much older traditional symbolism including pastoral motifs such as the sower or the Slovene hay-rack known as the *kozolec* and one of its 'ur-motifs', the Stag. From early cave art onwards, the Stag has been one of the most frequently used and powerful symbols, recurring throughout art history in Europe and beyond. This means that although it is often used in a kitsch / ironic way, its deployment can still trigger subconscious or pre-rational associations and it carries a primal charge.

Politically, it is strongly associated with hunting, and with what are characterized as anti-cosmopolitan provincial attitudes. This is certainly the way it is deployed in populist Austrian *Heimatfilme* such as *Der Förster vom Silberwald* (1954). It appears as a symbol of non-alienated traditional values. In Austria and to a lesser extent in Slovenia, outsiders generally view hunters who wear antler symbols on their clothing as an inherently reactionary group. The stag is a power symbol deployed by specific hierarchies and their client groups, i.e. rural populations who defend what are basically feudal relations. While it also appears as a symbol in contemporary contexts it is seen as being tainted by association with a value system antithetical to any contemporary art and culture, let alone ideas such as bruitism, Punk or performance art. Additionally, leaders such as Tito or Franz Ferdinand – who boasted of having shot 3,000 stags – have used the practice and symbolism of hunting as a symbol of political virility and the stag was traditionally seen as a royal animal. Thus, the Stag as a symbol always carries the metaphorical scent of blood, suggesting particular hierarchies and traditional practices and codes of honour. Therefore NSK's appropriation of it was as much a (symbolic) political challenge as its appropriation of state and ideological symbolism.

Who Doubts the Terrible Power of these Horns?
Construction of the New Acropolis

'LAIBACH and NSK analyzed nationalism through the aesthetic dimension. By placing "national and subnational" symbols alongside each other, we demonstrated their "universality". That is, in the very process of one nation defining its difference against the other, it frequently uses the same, or almost the same, kind of symbols and rhetoric as the other. In short, nations are not very original at all when it comes to defining their own originality – their *raison d'être* – against each other. Indeed, they often use exactly the same arguments and symbols (compare, for instance, the use of the eagle symbol by the

Germans, Americans, Albanians, Austrians, Poles, etc.). Paradoxically, then, nationalistic conflict between nations are usually not the result of differences, but because the differences are too small (for instance, only a few English people know that they're essentially an English-speaking Germanic tribe). Such nationalism is based on "the narcissism of small differences". It is the most popular, most European and most fatal. Also in the countries of ex-Yugoslavia.' – Laibach

See http://www.nskstate.com/laibach/interviews/excerpts-91-95.php

Given the extent to which it is bound up with representations of power, it should be no surprise that the stag has been central to NSK's iconography since 1982. Like all NSK's appropriated symbols, the stag is structurally paradoxical. NSK made it into a symbol of new Slovene art and subsequently of the NSK State in Time, but it actually began its symbolic journey in nineteenth century Scotland. The source of the stag that features most frequently in NSK visual art works is actually Landseer's famous painting The Monarch of the Glen (1851), an iconic Scottish image that appears in numerous commercial contexts such as Glenfiddich whisky and Campbell's soup packaging. It is interesting to note that NSK have always found an appreciative audience in Scotland, exhibiting there before London. There are certainly some similarities between Scotland's place in the UK and Slovenia's place in the old Yugoslavia – both being northern nations within larger multi-national states. NSK's appropriation of the monarch was in fact a sequel to Peter Blake's pop art version. Despite appearances pop art works and techniques were an important precedent for NSK. In this respect, 'there is no Slovene Stag' and this original foreign source points to the spectral nature of NSK's performance of national mobilization.

The 'Slovenization' of the monarch began in 1982 with the exhibition Ausstellung Laibach Kunst in Ljubljana, the first manifestation of what Laibach termed the 'monumental retro-avant-garde'. A reproduction of the monarch was featured surrounded by Xeroxed images of a monumental worker figure and the controversial name Laibach (the historic German term for Ljubljana). In this context, the monarch was conspicuous as a 'high art' retro presence within an aggressively contemporary multimedia installation. This temporal tension between ultra-traditional and ultra-contemporary is one of Laibach's most characteristic qualities and is intrinsic to what we can call the 'Laibach effect' – the generation of contradictory audience interpretations from the same source.

By the end of 1983, Laibach was performing in London at the end of the first stage of its first *Occupied Europe Tour*. Laibach performed an extremely challenging combination of industrial music with atonal classical elements and were a fixture on the international avant-garde scene. At a concert at London's Diorama venue, Laibach first placed a stag's head on stage. Although it was thrown into the audience during the show, stag's heads went on to become an expected element of every Laibach show during the 1980s. In some cases, antlers alone were used, sometimes attached to a Laibach painting. In other cases a full scale hunting trophy was used. The significance of this was that Laibach deployed something simultaneously *Völkisch*, ideological and primeval as part of contemporary culture, rendering the archaic contemporary and the contemporary archaic. This was exactly the type of allegedly reactionary symbolism that other alternative artists and musicians would see as untouchable. For Laibach it was an essential part of a strategy designed to make it seem more powerful and absolute than any 'actually existing' state could then be.

Its use also represented a sinister temporal dislocation; an allusion to what majority opinion likes to believe is a safely surpassed dark past. In the senso-brutalist *See my contribution entitled, 'The Evolution of Senso-Brutalism' in the English content section of www.skug.at* context of a Laibach concert the normally concealed power of the archetypal image is revealed, stripped of its normal reassuring 'folksiness, which Laibach reveals as being connected to force, terror and mobilization. Laibach's over-identification gave it (and themselves) more power than it actually possessed, aiding the construction of its own illusory power.

Here we have to acknowledge that there was also an element of fanatical absurdism present. British audiences in particular tended to view the antlers as proof that the entire spectacle was 'really' or 'primarily' a joke, and thus that it had no further implications. Some British reviews even reported that Laibach wore the antlers and seemed to need to emphasize the ludicrous aspects, as if they discounted the overall presentation. This overlooked the very real discomfort caused by Laibach's use of such symbolism, which is very far from the standard mocking position of many artists. In the Central European/Alpine context the stag is certainly a kitsch symbol but its use by Laibach seemed deadly serious because of its ongoing association with reactionary political forces.

However, the Stag was much more than a curious stage prop. The ambivalently titled 1985 live album *Neu Konservatiw* features another less placid Landseer image of a terrified drowning stag. The monarch appeared again on the cover of Laibach's 1986 album *Nova akropola*. This time with a cross between its antlers, an allusion to the legend of St. Hubert, patron saint of hunters. *Nova Akropola*'s literally exorcistic track *Vade Retro (Satanas)* also features a stag. From the midst of an extremely harsh sound field, the sampled call of a rutting stag emerges. Once again, the familiar symbol becomes associated with primeval terror and fascination, re-emerging as a force of nature as relevant and disturbing in 1986 as in 986. Many artists use natural references but what is present here is a natural archetype, more intimidating than welcoming and integral to Laibach's over-identification with 'eternal' values and laws. This also took the form of appropriating traditional Tyrolean style hunting clothes of a type now rarely seen in Slovenia but still present in Austria. Laibach even wore the insignia of the Slovene Hunting Association (SLD) and their videos feature Stag clips from hunting films. This hunting image soon drew fire from certain quarters and Laibach played out a more honestly reactionary role than actual hunters now tend to. Asked if they were aware of the animal rights movement they replied: 'We know about it, but the animals don't.'

This stance was also significant as it dramatized the fact that even under the modernity of self-management socialism, hunting motifs and Alpine symbolism remained present in Slovene culture, which despite the official emphasis on the 'Brotherhood and Unity' of the Yugoslav peoples still bore traces of its former Austrian rulers. Laibach's image in this period was more typical of southern Austria or Bavaria than of contemporary Slovenia, yet it paradoxically managed to transmit an internationalized Sloveneness via an excessive 'Germania'.

Alongside Laibach stood the other NSK groups, all of which used the stag or antlers as one of the symbolic building blocks of the *Gesamtkunstwerk* that eventually became the NSK State in Time. Indeed, antlers form a key part of NSK's insignia. The visual arts collective IRWIN took the Slovene stag and subjected it to an intensive process of multiplication, and continues to take it into new contemporary contexts. Representations of the Stag comprise an entire iconographic series in IRWIN's Icons project. See http://www.nskstate.com/irwin/works-projects/irwin-icons.php These stags are juxtaposed with incongruous elements such as Lego bricks or modernist motifs. The oppositions

**set up by the contradictory elements further complicate the status of the** Slovene Stag, further removing it from a directly national role. Additionally, many of their installations featured stags and other hunting trophies, creating the impression of a dislocated temporal space similar to Laibach's concert nvironments. Like Laibach, IRWIN takes the Stag both back to the classicist aesthetics of oil painting and European tradition and forward into the digital context. This is intrinsic to their original self-identified role as 'state artists' – a category that obviously disturbs those unable to accept the legitimacy of over-identification.

In 1986 NSK created its most monumental collective presentation, the performance *Krst pod Triglavom* (Baptism under Triglav). IRWIN provided the scenography and Laibach the music for the production by NSK drama group Scipion Nasice. Here again, Stags and hunting motifs were central to what would have seemed to outsiders to be an exercise in nationalist assertion. The reality is more complex. Krst's theme was the forced conversion and colonization of the pagan Slovenes by German forces in the ninth Century. It addressed the extent to which Slovene identity has been endangered and suppressed by its larger neighbours and the paradoxical possibility of asserting Sloveneness using international sources. Alongside the Slovene historical and mythological references, NSK employed the art of Kandinsky, Tatlin and Malevich and the Slovene 'historical avant-garde', the music of Kraftwerk, Bruckner, Liszt and more. Laibach were not only **reprocessing the German classical canon, but even Volksmusik. NSK successfully used the Germanic imagery and culture that traditionally dominated the Slovene space in order to transmit** the previously repressed culture within the heartland of the former enemy.

In this way, a small so-called 'unhistorical' culture of two million people symbolically assumed 'great power' status in the cultural sphere, insisting on its right to recognition while acknowledging the foreign influences upon it. Slovene culture and language have historically been known to very few foreigners and prior to NSK there was no precedent for its systematic international transmission. **Here we can see why some of NSK's harshest critics remain conservative Catholic nationalists who resent the linking of 'their' national symbols with foreign** and avant-garde sources. Over-identification has exposed some of the private national-folk power rituals that lose their kitsch innocence and effectiveness when exposed. However, we can also see why the *Völkisch* imagery made so dangerously credible by the Slovene Stag and other signifiers causes alarm. Yet the career of the appropriated and (inter)nationalized, multiplied and industrialized Slovene Stag is the clue that NSK is always also pointing away from what it seems to point unambiguously towards.

Progressive Alpinism?

The trajectory of the Slovene stag suggests that the presence of the archaic and the traditional are deeply embedded in the contemporary. Such symbols adapt and mutate to changing times and find new hosts and carriers.

In a sense, the 'New Slovene Stag' stands for everything over-identification implies: the refusal not to use tainted symbols. It is clear why this type of symbolism enrages many on the Left, but NSK's appropriation also affects the Right. For a further development of this idea, see Alexei Monroe, Full Spectrum Provocation – The Retrogarde Cultural Strategies of Neue Slowenische Kunst, Andere Sinema 176 (2006) Looking at it closely, it becomes clear how with the opulence and monumentality of its representations, NSK created an abstracted spectacle with which no actual state or nationalist manifestation could compete. In the Slovene context, NSK's appropriation of symbolism that would normally be used by government or far-right groups has been so complete as to alienate it from its natural constituencies. This type of appropriation can amount to a kind of counter-contamination that permanently stains its subjects. They are stained both with the normally concealed power associations and with their use by artists seen as decadent by many. The intensive repetition of motifs sustains the necessary illusion of fanaticism but in the process can dilute the actual fanaticism associated with them, taking them further from their original sources and complicating the enjoyment of those used to exercise a monopoly over them.

The foreign source of the Slovene Stag was paradoxically central to the way in which NSK (re-)invented the traditions of its own semi-fictional nation and then transmitted them internationally. It guaranteed an internal distance while presenting a monumental and threatening external façade that seemed to contain no distance whatsoever. This is central to the most aggressive forms of over-identification – there should initially seem to be no possible space for doubt, even though contradictory symbolism is present. Those confronted by it have to be left to work out whether there is any distance and of what type. Over-explanation has to be avoided and the possibility, even the probability, of misinterpretation has to be accepted. In fact, if the phenomenon does not at least some of the time appear to be what people most fear it to be then it will be less effective. To paraphrase Laibach, 'all interpretations must be correct' – the negative as well as the positive. Laibach's demonization as nationalists has sometimes worked as positive propaganda, amplifying the effects of its interventions. Over-identification means accepting the likelihood of being identified (only) with the most demonic aspects of the regime the technique is applied to and of being 'shot by both sides'. It should be 'red in tooth and claw', encoding painfully real elements of power and in the process alienating them from those who normally wield them.

Obviously there are risks associated with reprocessing the type of power symbolism intrinsic to over-identification, but it has to be asked whether abstaining from this is any less risky. The fact that symbols such as the Stag have been contaminated by the Nazis and others actually demands a counter-contamination. Many on the Left engage in a ceaseless *Kulturkampf* against this type of traditional European symbolism, claiming that any use of it – except perhaps the most contemptuously ironic – is unacceptable. However, they will not fade away because they are ignored or even criminalized by enlightened elites. In fact, this simply leaves a potentially powerful symbolic arsenal as the unchallenged property of the Right and makes plausible propaganda about progressive forces being intent on destroying all tradition. This censorious approach, which amounts to a refusal to 'get their hands dirty', is a colossal tactical error. There is no possibility of any non-aggression pact since both sides abstain from symbolic warfare. On this front there should, therefore, be no question of what amounts to unilateral symbolic disarmament. Here then is the challenge presented by the example of NSK: why should such symbolism not be taken deadly seriously as a legitimate weapon and why should 'we' not appropriate it for counter-cultural irregular use? Entire categories of imagery and tradition cannot be proscribed without generating massive opposition. The challenge is to find and construct non-reactionary modes of using and even respecting these categories. Why not a 'progressive Alpinism' as is already apparent in the work of the Austrian group Attwenger? By now there are enough examples of such reclamation and reprocessing strategies out there, and perhaps the time has come to stop talking and 'just do it!' This paper was presented as a lecture at the conference 'Cultural Activism Today. Strategies of Over-Identification'. Part of it is reworked in Alexei Monroe, Interrogation Machine: Laibach and NSK (Cambridge MA: MIT Press, 2005).

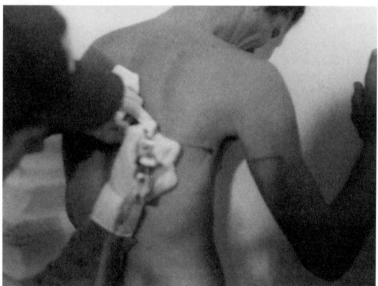

**Santiago Sierra, *250 cm line tattooed on 6 paid people*, Espacio Aglutinador, Havana (1999)**
Unemployed Cuban Youngsters having a line tattooed on their backs
in return for $ 30. *Copyright: Santiago Sierra and Lisson Gallery, London*

**Atelier Van Lieshout, AVL-Ville, installation, Rotterdam (2001)**
On an abandoned plot in the port of Rotterdam a free-state was decreed to experiment
with artistic freedom, anarchy and autarky. *Photo and copyright: Atelier Van Lieshout*

Christoph Schlingensief, *Bitte liebt Österreich!*, action, Vienna (2002),
still taken from Paul Poet's documentary *Ausländer Raus. Schlingensief's Container* (2005)
*Big Brother* show in which the Austrian people could vote asylum seekers off the
show and out of the country. *Copyright: Monitorpop Entertainment*

**EGBG – Martijn Engelbregt, *Regoned*, action, De Balie, Amsterdam (2004)**
An opinion poll mapping the willingness among the inhabitants of an Amsterdam
neighbourhood to report illegal residents. *Photo and copyright: Martijn Engelbregt*

**Santiago Sierra, *3000 holes of 180 x 50 x 50 cm each*, Montenmedio Arte Contemporáneo, Vejer de la Frontera (2002)** Three thousand holes of precise dimensions dug out on a slope near a luxurious holiday resort by African day labourers paid the minimum wage.

Christoph Schlingensief, *Bitte liebt Österreich!*, action, Vienna (2002),
still taken from Paul Poet's documentary *Ausländer Raus. Schlingensief's Container* (2005)
Big Brother show in which the Austrian people could vote asylum seekers off the
show and out of the country. Copyright: Monitorpop Entertainment

**Michael Moore, *Fahrenheit 9/11*, still taken from the movie (2004)**
Pro-war U.S. congressmen are encouraged to set a good example by sending
their sons and daughters to Iraq. *Copyright: Lionsgate Films*

**Christoph Schlingensief, *Bitte liebt Österreich!*, action, Vienna (2002),
still taken from Paul Poet's documentary *Ausländer Raus. Schlingensief's Container* (2005)**
*Big Brother* show in which the Austrian people could vote asylum seekers off the
show and out of the country. Copyright: Monitorpop Entertainment

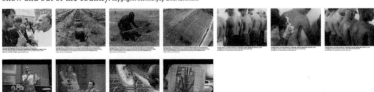

**Jens Haaning, *Superdiscount*, installation, Fri-Art, Fribourg (1998)**
By importing consumer items from France to Switzerland as art objects, visitors
to the gallery could acquire the goods up 35 % cheaper. *Photo and copyright: Jens Haaning*

# Artistic Over-Identification:
## Overrated or Underestimated? A Revaluation of Atelier Van Lieshout's Activism

by Benda Hofmeyr

> Atelier Van Lieshout: We make Money not Art!

The thirty odd members of the Dutch artists' collective, Atelier Van Lieshout (AVL) gather together their artistic and technical expertise to create individual pieces, which, in turn, can be put together to create organized forms of communal working and living that circumvent conventional categories. Their objective is twofold: their works should not only be practical but also practicable. Apart from being useful and fully functional, it should also be viable.

This twin objective is reflected in their projects of the last five years – from *AVL-Ville*, *Bonnefantopia*, *The Disciplinator*, *The Technocrat* through to *SlaveCity* (formerly known as *Call Centre*) – which can be seen as the successive stages of increased utility and viability. *AVL-Ville*, the 'free state' proclaimed in the port of Rotterdam, might have lasted only nine months, but its dream of autarky, of economic independence and self-sufficiency lived on in the projects that followed. Ironically, however, AVL seems to have sacrificed its libertarian aspirations in the process. *AVL-Ville* was an experiment in the creation of a sustainable self-supporting infrastructure that could generate its own power by recycling its waste products. Septic tanks and compost toilets were meant to convert excrement into electricity, which in turn would fuel the kitchen that feeds the faecal- and art-producing members of the self-contained community. But Van Lieshout felt that things could be done more efficiently.

What was needed was a human power plant, a meticulously orchestrated concentration camp designed to extract maximum profit from its 72 inmates: enter *The Disciplinator*. This gigantic cage-like structure is segmented into sleeping, feeding, working and sanitary areas. The 24 bunk beds are meant to be used in three shifts of four hours each, the table seats 24 people, and the labour camp has 36 places where inmates/inhabitants perform intensive labour tasks and produce sawdust from four tree trunks using the 36 files. Everything is meticulouslycalculated from the work hours to the number of toilets, sinks, showers, even the toothbrushes. Everything fits neatly into a rational scheme that translates into 'an unadulterated vision of the horrors of the principle of exploitation'. See http://www.we-make-money-not-art.com/archives/006382.php

For mastermind Joep van Lieshout this was not enough, however. 'Things can get even worse', he boasts, in the form of *The Technocrat*.

*These and other statements and descriptions of his latest work are taken from a lecture Van Lieshout gave during the symposium, 'Cultural Activism Today' in the Stedelijk Museum CS, Amsterdam on January 19, 2006.* *The Technocrat* was designed to replace and improve the waste disposal system of septic tanks and compost toilets operative in AVL-Ville. This more efficient waste recycling system consists in a biogas installation. Van Lieshout explains the genius of its simple mechanism: the faecal matter is placed in a container with oxygen and then heated; some bacteria are added and voilà: biogas! To maximize the yield, it is important to separate the excrement from the urine, Van Lieshout stresses. For this, one needs not only separate toilets but also a surveillance system of cameras and mirrors to check that people are doing what they are supposed to be doing where they are supposed to do it. The end product is an all-in-one art installation that manages to combine green (environmentally friendly) and control mechanisms beautifully!

In addition, the biogas installation includes a vacuum tank hooked up to one thousand hoses. These hoses in turn are meant to be hooked up to one thousands prisoners from which to extract the requisite faecal matter. But, of course, without any food there will be no excrement, which led to the need for another installation: *The Feeder*. And while food is important, it is not quite enough to keep the battery of prisoners happy and docile. *The Alcoholator*'s task is reminiscent of the doctor's who must watch over those condemned to death in Foucault's *Discipline and Punish*. He explains that '[w]hen the moment of execution approaches, the patients are injected with tranquillizers ... deprive the prisoner of all rights, but do not inflict pain'. *See Michel Foucault, Discipline and Punish, trans. Allen Lane (London: Penguin Books, 1977).* This installation is a graphic depiction of the twin task of maintaining life while draining it at the same time, a spectre of what Foucault described as 'an infinitesimal power over the active body'. An excessive but nevertheless exemplary incarnation of those 'disciplines', 'which made possible the meticulous control of the operations of the body, which assured the constant subjection of its forces and imposed upon them a relation of docility-utility'. Foucault continues: 'discipline produces subjected and practised bodies, "docile" bodies' ... it 'increases the forces of the body (in economic terms of utility) and diminishes these same forces (in political terms of obedience). In short, it dissociates power from the body; on the one hand, it turns it into an "aptitude", a "capacity", which it seeks to increase; on the other hand, it reverses the course of the energy, the power that might result from it, and turns it into a relation of strict subjection. If economic exploitation separates the force and the product of labour ... disciplinary coercion establishes in the body the constricting link between an increased aptitude and an increased domination' Ibid., 137-138.

According to Van Lieshout, *The Disciplinator* corresponds to or mirrors society, specifically the way in which 'human beings are reduced to a small particle in a giant machine'. AVL's most recent project, *SlaveCity* represents perhaps the most unmitigated incarnation of or identification with the disciplinary techniques Foucault wrote about in the 1970s. It consists in a larger scale forced labour camp designed to accommodate 200,000 inmates. It combines state of the art techno-logical innovation with the latest management skills for maximum profit.

It is at this point that one starts wondering whether AVL is not more interested in making money than art. While they are sticking to the ideal of a self-contained community, the emphasis has clearly shifted from 'free state' to money-spinner. *SlaveCity* is quite simply a super efficient, environmentally friendly human battery. Described by the architect himself as 'the largest zero energy settlement in the world with a minimum of carbon dioxide pollution', it operates by inserting human cells first into a call centre and then into the workshops or fields in two consecutive seven-hour shifts. In this way, all energy needs are met without the aid of imported mineral fuel or electricity. The rest includes an art centre, hospital, kitchen, education centres and brothels to cater to the secondary needs that support the primary function: to churn out profit. A sophisticated computerized monitoring system insures that the estimated 7.5 billion Euro profit margin is met annually. In short: a superlative business plan that uses subjugation, control and efficiency to ensure maximum profit.

It is difficult to know what to make of AVL's often incongruous exploits. Should we read something into the peculiar mix of communism and capitalism, of freedom and subjection, of anarchism and the oppressive top-down organizational structure of their latest work? Should we take seriously all their talk of 'weapons' or should we dismiss it as mere misplaced romanticism in a time in which the rest of us take artistic / cultural activism seriously? The general consensus is that AVL's projects operate as an ironic commentary on the ever-diminishing freedom of modern man in a technological society. *See* 8Weekly Webmagazine *on* http://www.8weekly.nl/index.php?art=2695 Perhaps that is giving them too much credit – or precisely not enough ... What if their attempts to find 'new ways to exploit people', their form of super-capitalism, their usurpation of the Other's discourse and methods contain the very means to subverting the Other? Before we can answer this question, however, we need to ascertain what it exactly means to speak the language of the Other, and when this strategy of over-identification simply reinforces the status quo instead of challenging it.

What is Over-Identification? Some Reflections From the Perspective of Foucault, Kant and Adorno

'... all art is subject to political manipulation, except for that which speaks the language of this same manipulation.' Third item of Laibach's covenant, see http://www.nskstate.com/laibach/texts/10items.php

Mimesis is a tactic often employed in art or literature to reproduce or imitate the real world. A mimic imitates to entertain or ridicule. In animal or plant life mimicry, resemblance or simulation serves to deter predators or protect against them through camouflage. However, speaking the same language does not merely mean repro-ducing or mirroring the ruling governmental rationalities. There seems to be something more at stake in over-identification than entertain-ment, derision or even survival – something akin to what Foucault called the 'critical attitude as virtue'. Michel Foucault, 'What is Critique?', in: Sylvère Lotringer and Lysa Hochroth (eds.), The Politics of Truth: Michel Foucault (U.S.: Semiotext(e), 1997) 25.

For Foucault, this critical attitude has bearing on the multiplication of the arts of governing, on 'governmentalization', which cannot be dissociated from the question 'how not to be governed?' This is not be understood as the opposite affirmation – that we do not want to be governed, that we do not want to be governed at all. Rather than opting for anarchy or asking how to become wholly ungovernable, Foucault's question is 'how not to be governed like that, by that, in the name of those principles, with such and such an objective in mind and by means of such procedures, not like that, not for that, not by them'. Ibid., 28. It is suggestive of a head-on confrontation or engagement, an act of defiance, 'as a way of limiting these arts of governing and sizing them up, transforming them, of finding a way ... to displace them, with a basic distrust'. This entails a 'cultural form, both a political and moral attitude, a way of thinking', which Foucault simply refers to as 'the art of not being governed like that and at that cost'. More than a mere gesture of rejection, it is the affirmative act of 'putting forth universal and indefeasible rights to which every government ... will have to submit'. Ibid., 30. If governmentalization is the movement through which individuals are subjugated in the reality of a social practice through mechanisms of power that adhere to a truth, then critique is 'the movement by which the subject gives him / herself the right to question truth on its effects of power and question power on its discourses of truth'. Ibid., 32. In short, critique has to do with power, truth and the subject. It has the power to 'ensure the desubjugation of the subject in the context of what we could call, in a word, the politics of truth'. Ibid.

Not everybody seems to be able to conjure up the critical attitude, to challenge the complex of relations that keeps the subject snug in the stranglehold of the power / knowledge noose. Kant even had a name for those who prefer to remain noosed and hooded, those who lack the resolution and courage to use their understanding without direction from another: the perpetually immature. Immanuel Kant, 'Was ist Aufklärung?', in: Lotringer and Hochroth (eds.), The Politics of Truth: Michel Foucault, 7-22. He explains: 'After the guardians have first made their domestic cattle dumb and have made sure that these placid creatures will not dare take a single step without the harness of the cart to which they are tethered, the guardians then show them the danger which threatens if they try to go alone'. Ibid., 8.

To Kant's injunction, sapere aude (Have courage to use your own reason! Ibid., 7.), Frederick II simply responded: 'Let them reason all they want to as long as they obey'. Ibid., 34. But what if excessive obedience becomes the very means to reason, critique, and finally to autonomy and freedom? What if fervent allegiance to the yoke – the very unwillingness to take a single step without the harness of the cart to which you are tethered – is the most effective form of insubordination? More than defiance it has the power to subvert the system of subservience, to lay bare the injustice of the yoke. Perhaps this is what Kant meant when he insisted that autonomy is not at all opposed to obeying the sovereign.

For Kant, freedom is paradoxically also a causality – a force that counters and frees us from an over-determination by the laws of nature. What he meant by freedom is 'simply this remarkable faculty that enables us to organize in our imagination the various components of the natural world or of existing reality, and to rearrange them in different ways from those in which we found them initially and in which they exist in reality ... this projecting element, this little piece of our nature that is not nature, is in actuality identical with consciousness of self'. Theodor W. Adorno, Problems of Moral Philosophy, Thomas Schröder (ed.), trans. Rodney Livingstone (Cambridge: Polity Press, 2000) 103. In short, 'we are no longer a piece of nature from the moment we recognize that we are a piece of nature'. Ibid. As soon as we take seriously our embeddedness in a certain formative context – be it the natural world or the existing socio-political reality – we become something more than the sum total of its formative influences. This is the moment at which the alienating force of critique kicks in, a force that disowns or dispossesses us from the very things that make us what we are and thereby sets us free. By fully embracing our imprisonment, we sign our release. We discover that we have been thrown into a world to which we do not belong, in which we are always-already forsaken and this *Heimatlosigkeit*, this exile, this *Da-sein* is the very key to a being standing apart and freed from an overdetermination by Being.

Kant's strength is to be found in his interlocking of freedom and law – the idea that an absolute freedom that is not also an intrinsically determined freedom amounts to the negation of freedom. For a condition in which there was no law at all would also be absolutely unfree, since everyone would be exposed to oppression at the hands of everyone else. This also holds for inner freedom: if people pander to their own needs without reference to reality and with no control over their own egos, they become dependent on themselves and therefore unfree. Think of an addict who cannot stop himself from satisfying his own needs even when they are incompatible with self-preservation. Ibid., 122.

This interlocking of freedom and law nevertheless remains a double-edged sword. Where law comes into play, freedom is exposed to potential attenuation. The law as an all-embracing regulation that tolerates no exceptions contains a totalitarian element especially if this constraint lacks the justification of reason. Where freedom is restricted it stands on a knife's edge, ready to vanish entirely. Even there where the sphere of law formally subserves the idea of protecting and guaranteeing freedom, it tends to abolish freedom. The relationship between freedom and the law is not the well-balanced, rational compromise that we would like it to be, but is a precarious balancing act between two dynamic sides. The law encompasses the instinctual energies of human beings. While these energies need to be contained, they should not be sublimated altogether. On the other hand, a psychological authority that is nurtured by sources of energy that have been separated off, like the super-ego, for example, runs the risk of turning into an absolute and to abolish freedom. We have to stay on our guard and remain constantly vigilant because the law tends to assert itself more effectively than freedom. Ibid.

In this context, Kant's call for courage – the courage to use your own reason – translates into having the audacity to confront the prevailing norms with your own consciousness and to measure each against the other. Kant takes natural consciousness as his starting-point. In other words, he begins with the moral intuitions that we all have. According to him, the moral law is a given that is present even in our ordinary consciousness and our task is to lay it bare. For Kant, to act morally is to act according to principles and to do so consistently. The problem today, however, as Adorno Ibid., 124. explains, is that present-day reality 'is so overpowering that it calls for agility, flexibility and conformity – qualities that rule out action in accordance with principles.' Kant's principles are predicated on a strong, stable self, something that no longer exists in that form. But what exactly does Adorno mean when he describes present-day reality as 'overpowering'? Elsewhere he complains about 'the immeasurably expanding universe of today which is incommensurable with our experience'. Ibid., 98. According to him, '[i]n the immeasurably expanded world of experience and the infinitely numerous ramifications of the processes of socialization that this world of experiences imposes upon us, the possibility of freedom has sunk to such a minimal level that we can or must ask ourselves very seriously whether any scope is left for our moral categories'. Adorno continues to flesh out his theory with an aesthetic analogy. He argues that as long as there had existed something like prescribed, established, given forms in music that corresponded to the prescribed, established, given forms of bourgeois life, it was possible for musicians to improvise. The less this was the case, the more these pre-established forms were eroded, the more the freedom of the artistic subject, and especially the freedom to improvise, was restricted. Ibid., 99.

Today, more than forty years after Adorno made his pronouncements, his diagnosis still holds. The literally infinite proliferation of neo-liberal power structures that has spread its tentacles on a global scale doing away with or rewriting rules and regulations in its own image – the image of a 'free market economy' – has virtually done away with freedom. Slavoj Žižek uses a slightly different idiom but in essence it reflects the same condition. According to him, the dominant attitude of the contemporary 'post-ideological' universe is precisely the cynical distance towards public values. In other words, this distance, far from posing any threat to the system, designates the supreme form of conformism because the normal function of the system requires cynical distance. See Žižek's 'Why are Laibach and NSK not Fascists?' on the Internet: http://nskstate.com/appendix/articles/why_are_laibach.php According to Adorno and Žižek, we live in a world in which freedom 'has shrivelled to the point of no return' Adorno, Problems of Moral Philosophy, 99. precisely because we maintain a cynical distance towards the law. The instances of the law that are still maintained are no longer inhabited by the World Spirit (as Hegel would have said) and can therefore no longer guarantee any freedom.

Žižek on Over-Identification

In a desperate effort to reclaim its ever-diminishing hold, the 'public' law has undergone a splitting or redoubling: 'Superego is the obscene 'nightly' law that necessarily redoubles and accompanies, as its shadow, the 'public' Law', as Žižek explains. See Žižek's 'Why are Laibach and NSK not Fascists?' To be sure, this splitting is not a new addition or incarnation of the Law but has always been an inherent and constitutive characteristic of the Law itself, but it is as if this 'underside', this private, shadowy side of the public law increasingly accounts for whatever effectiveness the Law might have in 'the immeasurably expanding universe of today'. Explicit, written, public rules do not suffice and need to be supplemented by a clandestine, 'unwritten' code aimed at those stubborn instances of recalcitrance that succeed in evading the long arm of the law – even though no overt violations are committed. 'The field of the law', according to Žižek, 'is thus split into Law qua 'Ego-Ideal', i.e. a symbolic order which regulates social life and maintains social peace, and into its obscene, superegotistical inverse'. Ibid.

Now, as we all know, periodic transgressions of the public law do not undermine it, but reinforce it and serve as the very condition of its stability. According to Žižek, however, there is more to it than that. He argues that what accounts for a community's cohesion is not so much identification with the Law that polices everyday communal life, but rather identification with a specific form of transgression or suspension of the Law. In psychoanalytic terms, this can be described as identification with a certain form of enjoyment. A community is held together by association with that obscene element, which supplements the overt law: the hidden reverse that contains the illicit charge of enjoyment.

It is in this particular crucible of clandestine exchange between the Law – which is publicly proclaimed and enforced – and superego –

which, as its obscene *Doppelgänger*, surreptitiously guarantees law-abidance – that over-identification comes into play. Over-identification drives the proverbial spanner in the works by bringing to light that which depends on the cover of night for its effectiveness. By exposing the obscene underside of the system, over-identification suspends its normal functioning. It causes unease by uncovering what we prefer not to see or acknowledge. Žižek explains how this works by referring to a 'homologous phenomenon in the sphere of individual experience': 'each of us has some private ritual, phrase (nicknames, etc.) or gesture, used only within the most intimate circle of closest friends or relatives; when these rituals are rendered public, their effect is necessarily one of extreme embarrassment and shame – one has a mind to sink into the earth'.

The avant-garde rockband Laibach, for example, which functions as the key reference in Žižek's theory of over-identification, effects an obsessive identification with totalitarian codes – taking totalitarianism more seriously than it takes itself. *See also Alexei Monroe's contribution in this volume, 49-57.* This strategy of fanatical identification succeeds in making manifest what usually needs to be suppressed for the social order to function unquestioned. It produces a contradictory enjoyment, a disruptive internal opposition. This would explain why the Communist authorities, in the face of the disintegration of socialism in Yugoslavia, did not embrace Laibach as mouthpiece or even applauded them as kindred spirits but banned their performances. Paradoxically Laibach's socialist mimicry did not reinforce the system (the ruling ideology) but upset the very dynamics necessary for its successful operation.

According to Žižek's analysis there is another mechanism at work in Laibach's strategy of over-identification that accounts for its subversive success, what he calls their 'deft manipulation of transference'. For Kant, 'Enlightenment' signals that moment in which we dare to use our reason, throw off the bane of tutelage and think for ourselves. In this supposed 'post-ideological age', we have not progressed much in terms of thinking for ourselves but are increasingly obsessed with what the Other thinks – with the 'desire of the Other'. Instead of providing us with an unambiguous indication of the Other's desire, over-identification functions, instead, as a confrontation, a question: what is the nature of your *own* desire? In other words, the indecisive nature of the desire of the Other, in this case that of the practitioners of over-identification, precisely forces us to start thinking for ourselves. In psychoanalytic terms, this signals the end of therapy, the dissolution of the initial transferential relationship in which the analysand sees the analyst as the subject-supposed-to-know, i.e. to know the truth about the analysand's desire. Transference is dissolved when the analysand comes to the realization that the analyst does not in fact hold the key to his/her desire, but deflects the question back to the analysand. The latter is then forced to acknowledge that his/her desire has no support in the Other, that it can only be authorized by oneself.

### Withstanding the Test: AVL's Status as Mechanism of Over-Identification

Let us recapitulate what we have learnt about over-identification. First, to qualify as a strategy of over-identification, the procedures implemented or devised by cultural producers must enact a certain public staging, a laying bare of what Žižek calls 'the obscene fantasmatic kernel of an ideological edifice'. This staging must succeed in suspending its normal functioning by creating a contradictory enjoyment. In other words, the re-enactment must create an excess, which undermines a straightforward association or affinity with it. It must produce unease or discomfort, which prevents us from enjoying it in an unambiguous way. Now, when we look at the tactics employed in works like *The Disciplinator*, *The Technocrat* or *Slave City*, which precisely consist in the public staging of capitalism's obscene underside – the total exploitation of individuals – the unease evoked is undeniable. Not even the most zealous champion of capitalism would be able to applaud without reserve such systematic depletion and replenishment of human batteries – whether it concerns 72 or 200,000 makes little difference. The more efficient AVL becomes in devising (artistic) methods of calculated exploitation, the less we are able to enjoy their schemes without a certain measure of mounting discomfort. We cannot enjoy it despite the fact that we are all inscribed in a profit-hungry economy, despite the fact that we are hungry for profit ourselves. Being obsessed with the desire of the Other, as we all are, we cannot refrain from asking ourselves, what if they really mean it? This brings us to the second criterion of over-identification.

Does AVL succeed in dissolving this transferential relationship and force us to start thinking for ourselves? Does their staging of a kind of super-capitalism, force us to take a stand, to acknowledge our own position in relation to our exploitative reality? Do they take themselves seriously enough to help us take ourselves seriously? It is at this point that their subversive potential begins to falter. In his lecture, presented during the 'Cultural Activism Today' symposium, Joep van Lieshout explained why AVL-Ville had to close down. One of the main reasons was that the people who worked on the project failed to commit to it completely, they were unable or unwilling to take it all the way – they worked there but were unwilling to erect a home and live there. AVL-Ville was not meant to function as a mere atelier or workplace, it was supposed to be a self-contained community, a home. AVL emulates the Shakers but they fail to 'walk the path', which perhaps explains why we as onlookers keep looking to them for answers without acknowledging that they are supposed to confront us with a question.

A crucial consideration remains to be accounted for. While the concept of over-identification might have been drawn from the armoury of psychoanalysis, it was forged by the cultural activists of the *Neue Slowenische Kunst* into a weapon against Tito's Stalinism. See also Alexei Monroe's contribution, 48-57. It was in the sphere of cultural activism that over-identification truly came into being in any meaningful sense of the term. The political potential of over-identification is therefore not something 'added on' as an adjunct. Rather, over-identification as such is intrinsically invested with political purport. It cannot be dissociated from a certain deliberate and determined activism, which in its analysis of the relation between art and ideology forges art into a weapon to uncover the ideological declension of our life world. In Foucault's words, the point is to '[u]se political practice as an intensifier of thought, and analysis as a multiplier of the forms and domains for the intervention of political action'. See Foucault's preface to the English edition of Gilles Deleuze and Felix Guattari's Anti-Oedipus: Capitalism and Schizophrenia, trans. Robert Hurley, Mark Seem and Helen R. Lane (Minneapolis: University of Minnesota Press, 1986) xiv.

So if the strategy of over-identification is indissociable from cultural activism, a third criterion needs to be added: it must purport to be an intentional action to bring about social or political change. This is Foucault's 'critique as virtue' in action – taking seriously the *how* in how not to be governed like that and at that cost. This is not about coming up with alternatives but about taking a firm stand, about claiming the inalienable right 'to question truth on its effects of power and question power on its discourses of truth'. Foucault, 'What is Critique?', 32 In other words, it entails a deliberate act of defiance against the existing forms of governmentalization. While AVL's projects testify to an awareness of the injustices of this world (exploitation, the depletion of natural resources) and represent clever strategies that use the product of exploitation (profit) to undermine the system of exploitation, they lack sincerity. *In his 'Cultural Activism Today' presentation, Joep van Lieshout argued that although the SlaveCity is premised on the very exploitation that it opposes, the profit generated can be used to change things for the better. The SlaveCity, he continued, also offers strategies to redress the depletion of our natural resources.* Joep van Lieshout unequivocally stated that if given the opportunity to realize *SlaveCity*, he won't do it. Behind their creative flirtations with capitalism, communism and anarchism, there is no clear position recoverable, no unambiguous desire, just a certain lingering immaturity. For all their creativity, they are incapable of real improvisation. This might have less to do with them than it does with 'the immeasurably expanded world of experience' in which we find ourselves. On the other hand, if taken seriously over-identification provides us with the very means we need to reclaim the law, which in turn makes possible a reclamation of freedom.

**Atelier Van Lieshout, The *Disciplinator*, installation (2003)**
Metal cage in which 36 inhabitants sleep, eat, work and defecate in shifts,
producing sawdust from four tree trunks using files. *Photo and copyright: Atelier Van Lieshout*

**Molly Nesbit, Hans-Ulrich Obrist, Rirkrit Tiravanija, *Utopia Station*, curatorial project, 50th Venice Biennale (2003)** Artworks are used by the curators as illustrations and documents of their vision of utopia. *Photo and copyright: Studio Armin Linke*

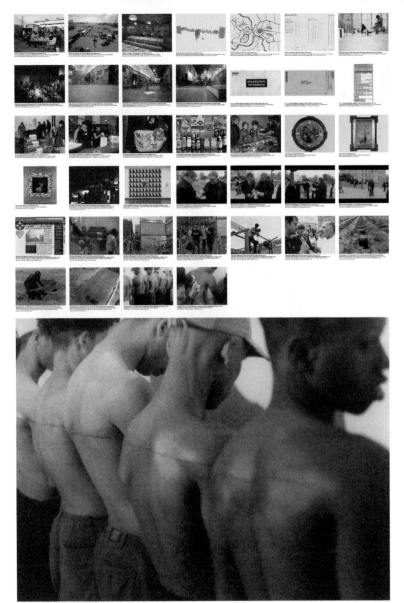

**Santiago Sierra, 250 cm line tattooed on 6 paid people, Espacio Aglutinador, Havana (1999)**
Unemployed Cuban Youngsters having a line tattooed on their backs
in return for $ 30. *Copyright: Santiago Sierra and Lisson Gallery, London*

**Irwin, *Deer*, mixed media (1988)**
Series of icons in which the symbol of the stag is juxtaposed
with modernist motifs. *Photo and copyright: Irwin*

**Red Pilot Cosmokinetic Theatre, *Drama Observatorium Zenit* (Hungarian version), theatre piece** (1990) Stage design of a science-fiction play in which mounted eagles and a stag are assembled together with modernist motifs such as Malevich's black cross.

Photo and copyright: Red Pilot Cosmokinetic Theatre

**EGBG – Martijn Engelbregt, *Regoned*, action, De Balie, Amsterdam (2004)**
An opinion poll mapping the willingness among the inhabitants of an Amsterdam neighbourhood to report illegal residents. *Photo and copyright: Martijn Engelbregt*

**Jens Haaning, *Superdiscount*, installation, Fri-Art, Fribourg (1998)**
By importing consumer items from France to Switzerland as art objects, visitors
to the gallery could acquire the goods up 35 % cheaper. *Photo and copyright: Jens Haaning*

**Molly Nesbit, Hans-Ulrich Obrist, Rirkrit Tiravanija,** *Utopia Station*, **curatorial project, 50th Venice Biennale (2003)** Artworks are used by the curators as illustrations and documents of their vision of utopia. *Photo and copyright: Studio Armin Linke*

**Mike Bonanno and Andy Bichlbaum, The Yes Men, action, still taken from the movie directed by among others Dan Ollman (2003)** Two anti-corporate activists lecturing on the latest developments in labour disciplining at an economic forum, posing as representatives of the WTO.

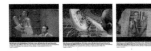

# Cultural Resignation Today:
## On Over-Identification and Overstatement
by Dieter Lesage

In *The End of History and the Last Man*, Francis Fukuyama holds the opinion that there is no place whatso-ever in present-day capitalist liberal democracy for cultural activism, either in the reformist or revolutionary sense of the word, not as intra-systemic nor as anti-systemic resistance. See Francis Fukuyama, The End of History and the Last Man, (London/New York: Penguin 1992). If we are to follow Francis Fukuyama, Ikebana is to be considered as the model for contemporary Western artistic practice. Since the end of history, art can only be a formal exercise. Of course the philosophical claim concerning the perfection of capitalist liberal democracy has been much contested ever since it has been made. In this essay, I will consider not one but two activist strategies in the cultural realm, which might very well be my own way to overdo it. Some cultural actors have acted in ways seemingly compatible with capitalist liberal democracy, where the excessive character of the systemic identification underlying these acts was supposed to destabilize the system. Other cultural actors have developed and spread a radical critical discourse that presents itself as a strategic alternative to capitalist liberal democracy. There is no doubt that what one could call the over-identifying act and the overstating discourse are indeed strategies. But one can doubt whether they are strategies of resistance. It is my thesis that it might be more appropriate to interpret them as strategies of resignation. In order to demonstrate this, I will consider two examples of cultural resignation today.

Let us first consider what I see as a clear example of the strategy of over-identification, albeit one that does not figure among the usual suspects. Alexandre Kojève, who, after the Second World War, had given up his Philosophy Chair in favour of a career as an official in the European Commission, would undoubtedly have been extremely pleased with Rem Koolhaas's much-discussed proposal for a new European logo – the so-called 'barcode flag'. See for instance, The New York Times (23 May 2002). After all, with Koolhaas's logo, which aims, by way of a branding strategy, to solve the problems of representation occasioned by the muddled, confederal character of the European Union, the formalism of Ikebana has, as Kojève predicted, eventually become a model for artistic practice. The role of the artist, or architect in this case, entails, at best, 'expressing' and shaping politics. The architect, who feels duty bound to add trendy logos to ponderous liberal-democratic institutions, is actually embracing Fukuyama's Ikebana-philosophy of art, despite all the rhetoric refuting it. Consequently, it is somewhat ironic that in 2003, Rem Koolhaas was the winner of the 15th *Praemium Imperiale* of the Japan Art Association. For AMO, Prodi was as much a client as Prada was. *AMO is the extraarchitectural counterpart to OMA (Office for Metropolitan Architecture), the architectural office led by Rem Koolhaas.* When the end of History is past, art and politics meet in discussions on the form of a multicoloured 'flag'.

Much of the work of the later Koolhaas can be considered as typical for a strategy of over-identification that does not contest the basic presuppositions of capitalist liberal democracy. One of these pre-suppositions is that politics should sell itself. Politics becomes a product in need of marketing strategies and Koolhaas is very eager to provide some ideas which, according to him, would help to sell the product. When Koolhaas suggests that the European Union should have a 'barcode' as 'logo', the European Union is supposed to identify itself as a product on a political market, where other products – for instance the nation-states – compete for a share. Clearly identifying oneself as a product on a market would contribute, according to Koolhaas, towards securing a respectable share in that market. Koolhaas's proposal presupposes the popularity of the market, or, to put it differently, the hegemony of neoliberalism. While many progressive European citizens and politicians would want to see the European Union as a chance, precarious though it may be, to contest neoliberalism, Koolhaas's whole endeavour is to popularize neoliberalism among progressive Europeans. Indeed, it seems much more certain that Koolhaas's 'logo-centrism' contributes to popularize market thinking among the European left, for which Koolhaas is somehow an icon, than to strengthen the share of a leftist view of Europe on the market of politics. Koolhaas has understood that for the left, the market may become acceptable through its aesthetization. Koolhaas is a master in aesthetization of the market, and therefore one of the greatest ideologues of neoliberalism.

Koolhaas's anthropology is diametrically opposed to that of Antonio Negri, whatever the mutual fascination both intellectual trendsetters seem to nurture for each other's work. *For Negri on Koolhaas, see for example: Antonio Negri, 'La moltitudine e la metropoli', in: Posse (October 2002).* For Negri, humankind is in the first place a producing animal, and production today is a cooperative venture. For Koolhaas, on the other hand, humankind is first and foremost a shopping animal and shopping is an experience that should be individualized as much as possible. While Negri, at the end of *Empire*, sings the praises of St. Francis, Koolhaas puts himself out in order to design a 25 million euro environment that would suit the exclusive shoes that Miuccia Prada has designed herself:

the so-called Prada Epicenter concept stores, like the one in Manhattan. Richard Heller, 'The House of Prada', in: Forbes (15 September 2003). While for Negri the metropolis is the place par excellence where the multitude can be mobilized against Empire, Koolhaas is eager to contribute to the expansion of the Prada-Empire. Or could it be that AMO, as an advisor on identity, branding and organization, has not seen that we have an Empire in the making here? The business policy of Prada-CEO Patrizio Bertelli aims at making Prada into a global multi-brand luxury firm that would soon bypass Gucci and LVMH, by buying large shares in other companies. Ibid. Within Negri's and Hardt's Imperial organization chart, Prada is an aggressive member of the aristocracy and operates on a transnational-elitist market. Nowhere do we find any semblance of a critical questioning by AMO of the predictable, unsophisticated commercial policies of Prada, nor of the place of Prada within Empire's organization chart. Apparently, AMO supposes that the artistic profile that Prada wants to give itself through the exhibitions in the Milanese Fondazione Prada and the state-of-the-art design of its Epicenter concept shoe stores is sufficient to turn the refined consumer into a Prada customer. It could also be that the raw business plan does not seem to matter much when it comes to the identity of the business in question. The simple fact that the respectability of important brands has been questioned in the past due to some aspects of their business plans raises questions concerning the ability of AMO to interpret their core business correctly. Unless it was Koolhaas's secret aim to make all Prada shops so ostentatiously expensive that in the global cities they would dethrone all McDonald's outlets as privileged targets of black bloc actions during antiglobal protests. Indeed, aren't handbags for the globeoisie more appropriate targets than hamburgers for the digitariat? For another critique on Koolhaas, see Hal Foster, 'Bigness', in: London Review of Books, vol. 23, n° 23, (29 November 2001).

The 'culture of congestion', which Koolhaas described and praised so acutely in his retroactive Manhattanist manifesto *Delirious New York*, seems to have been replaced by a proactive hyper-capitalist manifesto for the 'culture of indigestion'. See Rem Koolhaas, Delirious New York. A Retroactive Manifesto for Manhattan, (Rotterdam: 010 Publishers, 1994 [1978]). Miuccia Prada, rated among the five hundred richest people in the world, may very well have studied political science and been a contributing member of the Italian Communist Party during her rebel student period. She may even have found it groovy to organize a fashion show in the Paris headquarters of the French Communist Party on 12 October 2000. There is surely only one name for this dubious *entente* between the one-time critical Koolhaas and fortunate Prada and that is communist chic. Apparently, hyper-capitalist liberal democracy is so boring that communists become intrigued by luxury and luxury producers get a kick out of their own flirtations with communism. The flirtations with the luxury brand Prada has been a sour experience for the Parti Communiste Français: while national secretary Robert Hue still obtained some 8.7% of the votes in the French presidential elections of 1995, he only had 3.37% of the votes during the first round of the presidential elections held on 12 April 2002, significantly less than the other leftist candidates.

The alliance between a transnational elite and an equally transnational intelligentsia does not constitute the alternative hegemony that a desperate world should hope for. The monstrous alliance between AMO and Prada is nothing more than a painful illustration of the established hegemonic alliance between transnational capital and a transnational intelligentsia that, after many years of hard labour, 'has come to the conclusion that the time has come to have one's share of all things pretty and beautiful. At the same time, it illustrates capitalism's enormous creative capacity, i.e. its ability to recycle communism as an aesthetic, even as a discourse. Simply put, it has found a brilliant way to neutralize a critical discourse. It is sufficient to publicize critique in the form of expensive, voluminous, glossy catalogues in which interesting statistics warn those who can still afford these books against all the perils that threaten the world. It is unlikely that the seductively beautiful books that Koolhaas and his collaborators have produced during the last few years ever fall into the hands of the multitude to whom Koolhaas likes to refer. One can imagine that Koolhaas does not want to write a manifesto that could mobilize the multitude for a political project. Koolhaas has no interest whatsoever in the multitude, only in the masses that, everywhere in the world, go to the cities. Koolhaas anxiously keeps records of the growing number of inhabitants of world cities, but nowhere will you find a glimpse of hope that all these people in all these cities could be mobilized for a world that would be at once more equal and more free. Perhaps Koolhaas is not an excessive apologist for capitalism, as a certain reading of his 'Projects for Prada' would suggest. Perhaps 'Projects for Prada' should be understood merely as a survival strategy for OMA and perhaps, then, Miuccia Prada is merely the gallant and noble saviour of one of the world's most interesting architectural firms. In this case, the existence of 'Projects for Prada' tells us as much about the continuing precarization of cognitive labour, more specifically about the uncertain living conditions of all those digitarians who work for AMO and OMA, than about the seemingly unlimited financial resources of a company like Prada. The extent to which Prada can appeal to the aesthetic sensibilities of the OMA digitariat entails that the project is welcomed enthusiastically by the digitariat and is not perceived as a shameful submission. In the figure of the glamour proletarian, one can find this remarkable cocktail of precariousness and expensive taste. Therefore, the monstrous alliance between AMO and Prada tends to be legitimized by the glamour proletarian respectability of aesthetic excess.

Neither in the products for Prodi nor in the projects for Prada, over-identification – respectively with a representative of liberal democracy and with a representative of capitalism – has been a strategy to resist either liberal democracy or capitalism. In both cases identification has been a survival strategy and over-identification a supplementary strategy to justify to oneself and others the brutal fact that one has made compromises in order to survive, that one has been compromised by a system one loves to hate.

Let us now consider what I see as a clear example of the strategy of overstatement. If in recent years there has been one place where activism in the arts seemed to have returned, if it had ever disappeared at all, then that was the eleventh *Documenta*. From the start, *Documenta* 11 seemed determined to give voice to underglobal despair and otherglobal critique. Okwui Enwezor, the first African artistic director of the manifestation, considered 'Ground Zero' as a symbol of resistance, albeit understood as resistance against western hegemony. Okwui Enwezor, 'The Black Box', in: Documenta 11—Platform 5: Exhibition. Catalogue (Ostfildern-Ruit: Hatje Cantz, 2002) 42-55. According to Enwezor, many different discourses provided elements to elaborate this resistance in peaceful terms. *Documenta* 11 was eager to produce interactions between reflection and artistic practice. Therefore it departed from the home-loving, traditional exhibition concept. Enwezor, assisted by six co-curators, organized *Documenta* into five so-called 'Platforms'. The six co-curators of Documenta 11 were Carlos Basualdo, Ute Meta Bauer, Susanne Ghez, Sarat Maharaj, Mark Nash and Octavio Zaya. Before the official opening that took place on 8 June 2002 at several locations around Kassel, there were four conferences in other parts of the world, dealing with the central themes, conferences that would later result in as many publications. *Platform* 1 ('Democracy Unrealized') took place in the *Akademie der Künste* in Vienna and the *Haus der Kulturen der Welt* in Berlin. Platform 1 took place from 15-20 March 2001 as a conference series at the Akademie der Künste in Vienna and from 9-20 October 2001 as a conference series at the Haus der Kulturen der Welt in Berlin. See Okwui Enwezor, Carlos Basualdo, Ute Meta Bauer, Susanne Ghez, Sarat Maharaj, Mark Nash and Octavia Zaya (eds.) Democracy Unrealized. Documenta 11—Platform 1 (Ostfildern-Ruit: Hatje Cantz, 2002). Platform 2 ('Experiments with Truth: Transitional Justice and The Process of Truth and Reconciliation') was organized in the India Habitat Centre in New Delhi. Platform 2, a conference and film- and video programme, from 7-21 May 2001. See Okwui Enwezor, Carlos Basualdo, Ute Meta Bauer, Susanne Ghez, Sarat Maharaj, Mark Nash and Octavio Zaya (eds.), Experiments with Truth. Documenta 11—Platform 2 (Ostfildern-Ruit: Hatje Cantz, 2002). Platform 3 ('Créolité and Creolization') was a workshop on the West-Indian island of Saint Lucia. Platform 3 took place from 13-15 January 2002. See Okwui Enwezor, Carlos Basualdo, Ute Meta Bauer, Susanne Ghez, Sarat Maharaj, Mark Nash and Octavio Zaya (eds.), Créolité and Creolization. Documenta 11—Platform 3 (Ostfildern-Ruit: Hatje Cantz, 2003). Platform 4 ('Under Siege: Four African Cities – Freetown, Johannesburg, Kinshasa, Lagos') took place in the Nigerian megalopolis of Lagos. Platform 4, a workshop and conference, 16-20 March 2002. See Okwui Enwezor, Carlos Basualdo, Ute Meta Bauer, Susanne Ghez, Sarat Maharaj, Mark Nash and Octavio Zaya (eds.), Under Siege. Four African Cities. Freetown, Johannesburg, Kinshasa, Lagos. Documenta 11—Platform 4 (Ostfildern-Ruit: Hatje Cantz, 2002). This unfolding of the *Documenta* on different platforms was clearly meant to delocalize *Documenta* somewhat, in order to increase its commitment with global issues and break with the occidentocentrism of the arts world.

At the same time, a microphysics of the delocalizations performed by the different Platforms in the latest *Documenta* edition shows that *Documenta* 11 only partially succeeded in the promised deconstruction of occidentocentrism. The workshop on the island of Saint Lucia took place in the Hyatt Regency, a luxurious Spa & Beach resort, while the conference in the former Nigerian capital of Lagos was organized in the very challenging environment of the local Goethe-Institut. In both cases, delocalization will not have been a very confronting experience. A workshop on creolization at a luxurious beach resort hardly seems to be the ideal context to legitimize the hypothesis of discourse as resistance. Despite all the standard hotel rhetoric which would have us believe that Hyatt hotels – especially in the design of the lobby and the guest rooms – engage in a dialogue with local culture, a Hyatt hotel is not the most appropriate location to reflect on creolization. According to the meticulous record of the conference in its subsequent publication, none of the artists or intellectuals present seemed to have noticed the absurdity of the situation, at least not on record.

When one speaks of 'the choice' of Documenta 11, one will evidently be commenting in the first place on the selection of artists. But if one puts this arts manifestation in a political context, as Enwezor did, then one is allowed to test its strategy and to judge Documenta also on its non-aesthetic choices. Then one asks oneself what kind of courage was needed to withdraw with a select group of people into a luxurious hotel on a Caribbean island during a cold German winter week. Not only the exclusive location, but also the secluded character of the workshop contrasted strongly with the omnipresent rhetoric of 'meeting' and 'confrontation'. An expansion of the concept of responsibility inevitably leads to these kinds of questions. The inflated rhetoric of dislocation, diaspora and deterritorialization also challenges a critical observer to have a close look at the spaces that are being occupied in these operations. And then the dry verdict of the catalogue says: 'Hyatt Regency, Saint Lucia', or simply, 'Documenta moved to no man's land'. Behind the post-colonial paradigm we discover a transatlantic pleasure trip – arts business as usual.

In the Documenta 11 exhibition catalogue, Ute Meta Bauer rightly addresses the critique that Documenta should have been held in Kassel, but her description of the locations of the different platforms as 'the relevant sites' for the respective discourses should be disavowed as rhetorical if one takes into account the specificity of each location. Ute Meta Bauer, 'The Space of Documenta 11. Documenta 11 as a Zone of Activity', in: Documenta 11— Platform 5: Exhibition. Catalogue (Ostfildern-Ruit: Hatje Cantz, 2002) 103-107. Documenta 11 did not really engage with the places on non-western continents where its first four Platforms were hosted, but managed each time to find a comforting local western context. While the principled choice for a mutual articulation of reflection and artistic practice can very well be defended, one has to recognize that the consequences of the theoretical choices of Documenta 11 had not been thought through to the capillary ends of its organizing body. The discourse on resistance that Documenta 11 was striving for did not result in a type of organization that matched its discursive counter-thoughts. And it did not help that Documenta 11, despite all its approving nods towards anti-globalization movements, occasionally preferred to settle down in the kind of reunion locations that world leaders also prefer when they hold their summits. In 1976, G7 met in the Hyatt Dorado Beach Resort and Country Club on another Caribbean island, Puerto Rico, a favourite holiday destination of almost all American presidents since Eisenhower.

This critique of Documenta 11 differs radically from the critique that blamed it for being too much about discourse. The predictable grumbling by Jan Hoet, artistic director of Documenta 9, could give the impression that what was at stake with this Documenta was the classical conflict between theory and practice, between concept and form, between word and image, between reflection and emotion, between ratio and intuition, and that the curators of this exhibition had chosen theory, concept, word, reflection, ratio above practice, form, image, emotion, intuition. The conflict, however, that really characterized this Documenta, was not a conflict between theory and practice, but between resistance and resignation. The discourse of Documenta 11 was not just any kind of discourse; it was a discourse on resistance. Not only were there many contributions to the four Platforms dealing with resistance that preceded the exhibition, the essays in the exhibition catalogue also reflected mainly on the potentialities of the arts as strategy of resistance. Unsurprisingly, one of the most frequently cited books in those essays was Empire by Antonio Negri and Michael Hardt. Okwui Enwezor, 'The Black Box', in: Ibid., 45, 48; Sarat Maharaj, 'Xeno-Epistemics: Makeshift Kit for Sounding Visual Art as Knowledge Production and the Retinal Regimes', in: Ibid., 75; Ute Meta Bauer, 'The Space of Documenta 11. Documenta 11 as a Zone of Activity', in: Ibid., 106; Mark Nash, 'Art and Cinema: Some Critical Reflections', in: Ibid., 131, 136.

Even here, however, there was a gap between the discourse and the practice of the organizers. Anyone who takes Empire seriously knows that it is a communist manifesto. The authors resist any kind of representative politics as the organizing principle of society. The global multitude is capable, they believe, of organizing itself. That is not a modest claim. But what to think then of the fact that four out of seven Documenta 11 curators were quoting Empire with the utmost approval? Why did we not see anything like panic in the arts scene as it had to witness this communist putsch? And why, on the other hand, did our communist curators not put an end to all forms of fetishism in a scene that is perverted by speculation, a scene that is endlessly complicit when it comes to the financial capitalism that controls much of the flows that characterize Empire? Why did the apparent production of knowledge on Empire – and Documenta 11 was, according to Enwezor, all about the production of knowledge – not give rise to a reflection on the place of Documenta itself within the Imperial organigram, as a global interface between artists and gallerists, collectors, curators and museums worldwide – an interface whose function consists in organizing the global flows of artists, art works and capital? And the question then is whether Documenta 11 succeeded in generating a regime of flows that could be qualified as anti-Imperial. Defining Documenta in terms of the jargon of Empire should allow us to discover whether Documenta 11 was merely flirting with philosophical hype, or whether its curatorial team were very serious about the Anti-Imperial critique of its representative majority's favourite book. The intellectual credibility of Documenta 11 would then depend upon the political principles that determined the organization of the flows I mentioned.

Some of the flows I have been describing give rise to the suspicion that Empire was mainly valued by the Documenta team for its theoretical hipness factor. The authors cannot help it that their book became a phenomenon. But one can judge the users of the book on the seriousness of their use. And one can seriously doubt this seriousness. In the Documenta 11 catalogue, from time to time, the word 'multitude' is ceremoniously quoted, but 'the multitude' is nothing to do ceremoniously about. As, for example, by Ute Meta Bauer, 'The Space of Documenta 11. Documenta 11 as a Zone of Activity', in: Ibid., 106. The concept figures, as we know, in Negri's and Hardt's radical critique of representative democracy. This theoretical context does not seem to have bothered the Documenta 11 curators much, though. Documenta remains an initiative of representative democracy, with all the pomp and ceremony it entails. As ceremoniously as its anti-representative multitudinarian rhetoric, the Documenta 11 catalogue's preface was signed by Georg Lewandowski, mayor of Kassel.

Therefore, the problem with Documenta 11 was certainly not that it was 'too political', as some have argued. The problem with Documenta 11 was that it was not political enough. The decision to situate an arts manifestation resolutely within the world, as the catalogue's visual introduction made clear – not without pathos – was a strong one. In spite of this, the discourse on this decision was evasive. It avoided the further choices that should have followed logically from this first choice. And thus it happened that the critique of capitalism scattered throughout the catalogue essays was soon to be replaced by praise for post-colonialism. Once again, the problematic of globalization was culturalized, even if Empire, the Documenta 11 curators' cult book, was quite blunt about the shortcomings of post-colonial theory. Again, this was no problem for the curators, who were having fun mixing Negri and Bhabha. One consequently has an odd impression when reading many of the texts in the catalogue and some interventions on the different platforms. Many of these pronouncements are theoretically incoherent, but nevertheless a virtuoso *métissage* of theoretical concepts and approaches. One could even risk the hypothesis that the kind of theory that is generally produced in the margins of the arts industry is a kind of academic creole, a language in which concepts from very different intellectual traditions are mixed. Academics, then, owe their legitimacy within the artistic community to their over-identification with artistic recipes. One could call many of the theoreticians that entertain the discourse parts of arts manifestations TJ's – theory jockeys.

There is in fact another more empathetic reading of Documenta 11 possible than the severe verdict of theoretical incoherence. This reading would proceed as follows: if the curators were conscious of these kinds of ambiguities, then they were apparently not capable of solving them organizationally. Instead they proceeded to supplement an event with a discourse, without the principles of that discourse being able to determine the organization of the event. If we demand from the organizers of the event intellectual coherence – a coherence that in many places was missing – then we fail to recognize that a mega-manifestation like Documenta allows curators, as much as it allows artists, nothing more than a chance to intervene superficially in a context already overdetermined before they enter the scene. The organizers cannot get a grip on the event and limit themselves to skirmishes in the margins. These skirmishes, which took the form of extra-territorial Platforms, seem to prefer the mode of discourse. A possible explanation for all this discursive audacity, for all this communist daring during all those Platforms, is that discourse is experienced as the site to which resistance had to withdraw. Consequently, resistance today is experienced as something, which is only possible as discourse. And if discourse is already considered a failure of resistance beforehand, then one might want to mask that failure by making the discourse stronger than is reasonable. The over-statement consequently becomes a strategy to experience resistance even within discourse. In this sense, the discourse on 'the multitude' sometimes seems to be characterized by the pleasure to be able to put all power in the hands of the multitude, at least in discourse, even if, or precisely because in the world as we know it, things are much more complex.

Considering the political deadlock of cultural strategies of over-identification and strategies of overstatement, one might wonder what was wrong with identifications and with statements in the first place. Politics begins with one's identification with a cause

and politics works through the translation of this cause into statements.
Any time one overdoes either the
identification or the statement, the cause tends to
get lost. When one sees how many so-called cultural activists make
sure that their cause gets lost, one may begin to think: *we have
never been political*. And this may very well be the ultimate goal of both
the strategies of over-identification and of overstatement. Self-defeating
as they are, they are excellent strategies in order not to be political
at all. This paper was presented as a lecture at the conference 'Cultural Activism Today. Strategies of
Over-Identification'. Part of it is based on a translation and adaptation from a section of my book Vertoog
als verzet. Politiek in tijden van globalisering (Amsterdam/Antwerp: Meulenhoff/Manteau, 2004).

**EGBG – Martijn Engelbregt, *Regoned*, action, De Balie, Amsterdam (2004)**
An opinion poll mapping the willingness among the inhabitants of an Amsterdam
neighbourhood to report illegal residents. *Photo and copyright: Martijn Engelbregt*

**Molly Nesbit, Hans-Ulrich Obrist, Rirkrit Tiravanija, *Utopia Station*, curatorial project, 50th Venice Biennale (2003)** Artworks are used by the curators as illustrations and documents of their vision of utopia. *Photo and copyright: Studio Armin Linke*

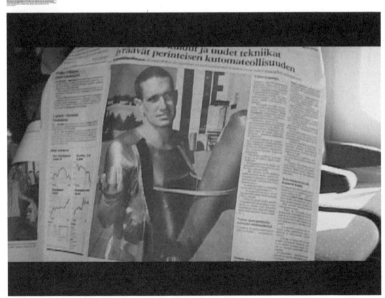

Mike Bonanno and Andy Bichlbaum, *The Yes Men*, action, still taken from the movie directed by among others Dan Ollman (2003) Two anti-corporate activists lecturing on the latest developments in labour disciplining at an economic forum, posing as representatives of the WTO.

**Santiago Sierra, *3000 holes of 180 x 50 x 50 cm each*, Montenmedio Arte Contemporáneo, Vejer de la Frontera (2002)** Three thousand holes of precise dimensions dug out on a slope near a luxurious holiday resort by African day labourers paid the minimum wage.

Copyright: Santiago Sierra and Lisson Gallery, London

**Michael Moore, *Fahrenheit 9/11*, still taken from the movie (2004)**
Pro-war U.S. congressmen are encouraged to set a good example by sending their sons and daughters to Iraq. *Copyright: Lionsgate Films*

**Jens Haaning, *Trade Bartering*, installation, Kunstnernes Hus, Oslo (1996)**
By importing consumer items from Denmark to Norway as art objects, visitors could
acquire the goods up to 40 % cheaper. *Photo and copyright: Jens Haaning*

**Molly Nesbit, Hans-Ulrich Obrist, Rirkrit Tiravanija, _Utopia Station_, curatorial project, 50th Venice Biennale (2003)** Artworks are used by the curators as illustrations and documents of their vision of utopia. Photo and copyright: Studio Armin Linke

**Santiago Sierra, *3000 holes of 180 x 50 x 50 cm each*, Montenmedio Arte Contemporáneo, Vejer de la Frontera (2002)** Three thousand holes of precise dimensions dug out on a slope near a luxurious holiday resort by African day labourers paid the minimum wage.

*Copyright: Santiago Sierra and Lisson Gallery, London*

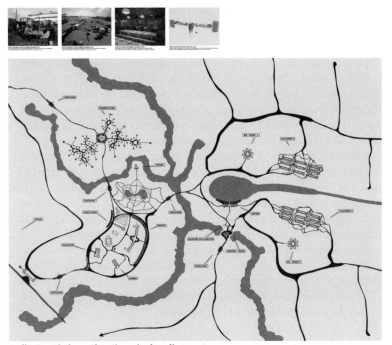

**Atelier Van Lieshout, *Slave City*, mixed media (2005)**
A forced labour camp for 200,000 inmates combining state of the art technological innovation with the latest management skills for maximum profit. *Photo and copyright: Atelier Van Lieshout*

# The Politics of Equal Aesthetic Rights
by Boris Groys

Art and politics are connected in one fundamental respect: both are realms in which a struggle for recognition is being waged. As defined by Alexander Kojève in his commentary on Hegel, this struggle for recognition surpasses the usual struggle for the distribution of material goods, which in modernity is generally regulated by market forces. What is at stake here is not merely that a certain desire is satisfied but that it is also recognized as socially legitimate. Whereas politics is an arena in which various group interests have, both in the past and the present, fought for recognition, artists of the historical avant-garde have contended for the recognition of all individual forms and artistic procedures that were not previously considered legitimate. Indeed, the historical avant-garde has opened up the potentially infinite horizontal field of all possible real and virtual forms endowed with equal aesthetic rights. One after another, so-called primitive imagery, abstract images and simple objects from everyday life have all acquired the kind of recognition that once only used to be granted to certain privileged images and objects.

Both forms of struggle for equality – political and aesthetic – are intrinsically connected to each other, and both aim to achieve a situation in which all people with their various interests, as indeed also all forms and artistic practices, will finally be granted equal rights. It is evident, however, that such a condition of total equality has de facto never been attained, neither in the political nor in the artistic realm. Contemporary art, like contemporary politics, still operates in the gap between formal equality and factual inequality. So the question arises: what are the mechanisms of this inequality – how can we define them and deal with them if we want to keep the promise of equality given by the historical avant-garde? As the avant-garde started its struggle against aesthetic inequality, it was the museum that was considered as the main enemy, as a place of inequality par excellence. The museums were perceived as guardians of the old privileges, as the places of the romantic iconophilia admiring the masterpieces of the past and preventing the emergence of the new, as the churches of the new religion of art with its strange rituals and esoteric conventions – closed spaces where the initiated few decided the fate of art beyond any democratic discussion and control. Accordingly, the avant-garde understood itself as an iconoclastic movement, as an attempt to secularize and democratize art in the name of equal aesthetic rights. Such appeals and demands have meanwhile become quite commonplace, even to the extent of now being regarded as a cardinal feature of contemporary art. Of course they remain in many ways legitimate. But the question arises: is the museum also today the central place of contemporary iconophilia and the origin of contemporary aesthetic inequality? Or: is the struggle that is directed against the museum – and the art institutions connected with the museum – truly iconoclastic under the contemporary aesthetic regime? Personally, I doubt it.

In the nineteenth and the first part of twentieth century, the socially dominating tastes were indeed defined and embodied by the museum. The criteria on which the museum based its choice of 'good' art were generally accepted as the aesthetic norm. But today it is simply not the case any more. Under the dominating aesthetic regime the museum has indisputably been stripped of its normative role. In our time it is the globalized mass media that dictate aesthetic norms, having long since dethroned the museum from its position of aesthetic dominance. The general public now draws its notion of art from advertising, MTV, video games and Hollywood blockbusters. The contemporary mass media has emerged as by far the largest and most powerful machine for producing and distributing images – vastly more extensive and effective than the contemporary art system. We are constantly fed with images of war, terror and catastrophes of all kinds, at a level of production with which the individual artist with his or her artisan skills cannot compete. Nowadays, every major politician, rock-star, TV-entertainer or sport hero generates thousands of images through his / her public appearances – much more than any living artist could ever imagine. The dominating aesthetics of our time is the aesthetics of the commercialized mass media – not of the museum.

In the context of contemporary, media-generated tastes, this means that the call to abandon and dismantle the museum has taken on an entirely different meaning than when it was voiced during the avant-garde era. Nowadays this protest is no longer part of the struggle waged against prevailing normative tastes in the name of aesthetic equality, but is – inversely – aimed at stabilizing and entrenching prevailing tastes. Characteristically, it is the gurus of the contemporary neo-liberal media markets who wonder today – in the style of the early avant-garde – why anyone at all is needed to decide what art is and what it is not. Why can't we just choose for ourselves on the open markets what we wish to acknowledge or appreciate as art without patronizing advice from curators and art critics? Why does art refuse to seek legitimation

on the open media market just like any other product? From a perspective of the media market the traditional aspirations of the
museum seem historically obsolete, out-of-touch, insincere and even
somewhat bizarre.

The strategies that are operating behind museum collections and
exhibitions are generally treated in the mass media as the workings
of a shadowy conspiracy, as an intrigue masterminded by insiders,
as a display of the hidden power of curators and museum directors
far removed from any form of democratic legitimation – in other
words, as an impenetrable swindle. Instead, the artists are invited
to follow the enticements of the mass media age, in the quest to
be disseminated through media channels. This enables them to address
and to seduce a much larger audience; it is also a decent way of earning
money, which the artist previously had to beg for from the state
or private sponsors. The mass media gives the artist a new sense
of power, social relevance and public presence within his or her
own time. However, this precisely means that the critique of the museum
has today lost its avant-garde edge. Instead, the call to break
loose from the museum amounts de facto to a call to medialize and
commercialize art by accommodating it to the aesthetic norms
generated by today's media.

At the same time, the mass media also appears at first as a new space
for the true art that was in a certain sense betrayed by contemporary
art as a result of its quest for the equal aesthetic rights. Certain images
circulating in the media become the icons of contemporary aesthetic
and political imagination not only because they are easily accessible,
almost omnipresent and conform to the prevailing aesthetic taste,
but in the first place because they are regarded as being real and true –
true precisely in the very old romantic, iconophilic sense. Kojève
already pointed out that the moment when the overall logic of equality
underlying individual struggles for recognition becomes apparent,
it creates the impression that these struggles have to some extent sur-
rendered their true seriousness and explosiveness. This is why Kojève
was able to speak of the end of history even before World War II – in
the sense of the end of the political history of struggles for recognition.
Since then, the discourse about the end of history has made its mark
particularly on the art scene. People are constantly referring to the
end of art history, with which they mean that these days all forms and
things have 'in principle' already obtained the right to be considered
works of art. Accordingly, the aesthetic equality of all images
that modern art has fought to establish is now frequently considered
as a sign of their arbitrariness and irrelevance. For if, as is argued,

all images are already acknowledged as being of equal value, this would deprive the artist of the possibility to create the images that could break taboos, provoke, shock or extend the boundaries of art. Instead, by the time history has come to an end each artist will be suspected of producing just one further arbitrary image among many. Were this indeed the case, the regime of equal rights for all images would have to be regarded not only as the telos of the logic followed by the history of art in modernity, but also as its terminal negation. Accordingly, we now witness repeated waves of nostalgia for a time when individual works of art were still revered as eminently precious, unique and singular because of being in some emphatic sense true.

Under these new conditions in which the whole musealized art has seemingly lost its seriousness and its claim to be true, it is the media that become the space where the quest for the true art takes place. In today's world the images of terror and of the war against terror function primarily as such true images – as authentic icons of the contemporary political sublime. Especially video art became the medium of choice for the contemporary warriors – and because of that the medium of truth. As we know, Bin Laden communicates with the outer world primarily by the means of this medium: we know him first and foremost as a video artist. The same can be said about the videos representing beheadings, confessions of the terrorists, etc. In all these cases we are dealing with consciously and artistically staged events that have their own easily recognizable aesthetics. Here we have people who do not wait for an artist to represent their acts of war and terror: they do not wait for a new Goya or a new Picasso. Instead, the act of war itself coincides with its documentation, with its representation. The traditional function of art as a medium of representation, and the role of the artist as a mediator between reality and memory are here completely eliminated. The same can be said about the famous photographs and videos from the Abu-Ghraib prison in Baghdad. These videos and photographs demonstrate an uncanny aesthetic similarity with alternative, subversive European and American art and filmmaking of the 1960s and 1970s. The iconographic and stylistic similarity is striking, to say the least. Think, for example, of Viennese Actionism or Pasolini movies. In both cases the goal is to reveal a naked, vulnerable, desiring body that is habitually covered by the system of social conventions. But, of course, the subversive art of the 1960s and 1970s aimed to undermine the traditional set of beliefs and conventions dominating the artist's own culture. In the Abu-Ghraib art production this goal was, we can safely say, completely perverted. The same subversive aesthetics was used to attack and to undermine another, different culture in an act of violence, in an act of humiliating

the other instead of questioning the self, thereby leaving the conservative values of the own culture unquestioned. But in any case
it is worthwhile to mention that on both sides of the war on terror the
image production and distribution are effectuated without any intervention by an artist. Here political action becomes synonymous with
artistic, aesthetic action – without any need for an additional artistic
practice of aesthetization.

At this juncture, I leave aside all the ethical and political considerations
and evaluations of this image production since I believe them to
be more or less obvious. It is important to stress at this point that we
are here dealing with images that became the icons of the contemporary
collective imagination. The terrorist videos and the videos from the
Abu-Ghraib prison are impregnated in our consciousness or even
sub-consciousness much more deeply than any work of any contemporary artist. This elimination of the artist from the practice of image
production is especially painful for the art system because artists –
at least since the beginning of modernity – wanted to be radical,
daring, taboo-breaking, transgressing all limitations and borders.
The avant-garde art discourse makes use of many concepts from
the military sphere, including the notion of the avant-garde itself.
There is talk of exploding norms, destroying traditions, violating
taboos, practicing certain artistic strategies, attacking the existing
institutions etc. The artists of the classical avant-garde saw themselves
as agents of negation, destruction, eradication of all traditional institutions of art. In accordance with the famous dictum 'negation is
creation', which was inspired by the Hegelian dialectic and propagated
by authors such as Bakunin or Nietzsche under the title of 'active
nihilism', avant-garde artists felt themselves empowered to create the
new icons by destroying the old ones. A modern work of art was
measured by how radical it was, how far the artist had gone in destroying
artistic tradition. Although modernity itself has meanwhile been
declared passé often enough, to this very day this criterion of radical-
ness has lost nothing of its relevance to our evaluation of art. The
worst thing that can be said of an artist continues to be that his or her
art is 'harmless'.

Along these lines, Don DeLillo writes in his novel *Mao II* that terrorists
and writers are engaged in a zero-sum game: by radically negating
that which exists, both wish to create a narrative which would
be capable of capturing society's imagination – and thereby altering
society. In this sense, terrorists and writers are rivals – and, as DeLillo
notes, nowadays the writer is beaten hands down because today's
media use the terrorists' acts to create a powerful narrative with which

no writer can contend. But, of course, this kind of rivalry is even more obvious in the case of the artist as in the case of the writer. The contemporary artist uses the same media as the terrorist or the warrior: photography, video, film. At the same time, it is clear that the artist cannot compete with the terrorist in the field of radical gesture. In terms of symbolic exchange, operating by the way of potlatch, as it was described by Marcel Mauss or by Georges Bataille, that means that in terms of the iconoclastic rivalry understood as the rivalry in destruction and self-destruction, art is obviously on the losing side.

It seems to me that this increasingly popular way of comparing art and terrorism, or art and war is fundamentally flawed. I will proceed by trying to show where I see the fallacy. The fact of the matter is that terrorism is not iconoclastic. Quite on the contrary: terrorism and war are extremely iconophilic practices. Indeed, the terrorist's or the warrior's image production aims to produce strong images – the kind of images that we would tend to accept as being 'real', as being 'true', as being the 'iconic revelations' of the hidden, terrible reality that is for us the global political reality of our time. I would say that these images are the icons of the contemporary political theology that dominates our collective imagination. These images answer the postmodern iconophilic nostalgia for a true image and at the same time they draw their power, their persuasiveness from a very effective form of moral blackmail.

After so many decades of modern and postmodern criticism of the image, of mimesis, of representation we feel somewhat ashamed to say that the images of terror or torture are not true, not real. We cannot say that these images are not true, because we know that these images testify to a real loss of life – a loss of life that is documented by these images. René Magritte could easily say that a painted apple is not a real apple or that a painted pipe is not a real pipe. But how can we say that a videotaped beheading is not a real beheading? Or that a videotaped ritual of humiliation in the Abu-Ghraib prison is not a real ritual? After so many decades of the critique of representation directed against the naive belief in photographic and cinematic truth, we are now ready to accept certain photographed and videotaped images as unquestionably true, again.

Here we are confronted with a strategy that is historically quite new. Indeed, the traditional warrior was interested in images that would be able to glorify him / her, to present him / her in a favourable, positive, attractive way. And we, of course, have accumulated a long tradition of criticizing and deconstructing such strategies of pictorial idealization. But the pictorial strategy of the contemporary warrior is a strategy of shock and awe. And it is, of course, only possible after the long history of modern art producing images of angst, cruelty and disfiguration. The traditional critique of representation was driven by a suspicion that there must be something ugly and terrifying hidden behind the surface of the conventional idealized image. The contemporary warrior shows us precisely this hidden ugliness, the image of our own suspicion, of our own angst. And precisely because of that, we feel ourselves immediately compelled to recognize these images as being true. We see things that are bad, as bad as we expected them to be – maybe even worse. Our worst suspicions are confirmed. The hidden reality behind the image is shown to us as being as ugly as we expected it to be. So we have a feeling that our critical journey has come to its end, that our critical task is completed, that our mission as critical intellectuals is accomplished. Now that the truth of the political has revealed itself, we can contemplate the new icons of the contemporary political theology without a need to go further. These icons are terrible enough by themselves. It makes no sense any more to criticize them in aesthetic terms; it suffices to comment on them. That explains the macabre fascination evident in many recent publications dedicated to the images of war on terror emerging on the both sides of the invisible front.

This also means that the source of contemporary iconophilia is not the museum but the mass media. The struggle of the avant-garde against the museum can be properly understood only by keeping that in mind. In fact, art became art originally through iconoclastic practice – through the iconoclastic practice of curators rather than artists. The first art museums came into existence at the turn of the nineteenth century, and became established in the course of the nineteenth century as a consequence of revolutions, wars, imperial conquest and pillage of non-European cultures. All kinds of 'beautiful' functional objects, which had previously been employed for various religious rituals, dressing the rooms of power or manifesting private wealth, were collected and put on display as works of art, that is, as defunction-alized, autonomous objects of pure contemplation. The curators administering these museums 'created' art through iconoclastic acts directed against traditional icons of religion or power, by reducing these icons to mere artworks. Art was originally conceived as 'simply' art. This perception is situated within the tradition of the European Enlightenment, which conceived of all religious icons as 'simple things'– as mere artworks. But the same should also be said about the icons of the contemporary mass consciousness. They are simply certain images among other images – nothing more. The art of today can keep its promise of equality of all images only by secularizing the icons of the present-day neo-liberal and pseudo-democratic, . populist media in the same way as it did with the old icons of religion and power. And by doing so one should not to be afraid to be accused of being elitist and undemocratic. The requirement of aesthetic equality of all images is namely much more radical than the requirement of the democratic, popular legitimization of certain images by the will of the majority. Also an allegedly democratically legitimized image is just an image – even if it is functioning as an icon of the mass media. Given our current cultural climate the art museum is practically the only place where we can actually step back from our own present and compare it with other historical eras. The museum is namely a place where we are reminded of tradition, of secularization, and of radical egalitarian art projects of the past – so that we can measure our own time against them.

Of course, museums cannot be places where all possible images are exhibited on a basis of perfect equality. The space of a museum is always limited. That leads to a selection of exhibited images by a curator – a selection that is always questionable and must be questioned. But the work of a curator is not primarily an act of selection. As I tried to show, in our time the work of selection is effectuated by the mass media – not by the museum curators. The work of a curator is an act of presentation – the act of presentation that presents itself. That is the central difference between the museum on one side and globalized media and art market on the other side. The curator cannot but place, contextualize and narrativize works of art, which necessarily lead to their iconoclastic relativization. The museum makes the act of showing, exhibiting and curating images visible. The art and media markets, on the other hand, conceal it, thereby creating the illusion of the autonomy of the image. The museum is a place where the act of curating becomes obvious – even if many curators try to reduce their curating to non-curating, to zero-curating in the tradition of Romantic iconophilia.

Giorgio Agamben defines the image as a being that in its essence is appearance, visibility or semblance. But this definition of the artwork's essence does not suffice to guarantee the visibility of a concrete artwork, however. A work of art cannot in fact present itself by virtue of its own definition and force the viewer into contemplation.

Artworks lack vitality, energy and health. They are genuinely sick and helpless – in the museum a spectator has to be led to the artwork, as hospital workers might take a visitor to see a bedridden patient. It is no coincidence that the word 'curator' is etymologically related to 'cure'. Curating is curing. The process of curating cures the image's powerlessness, its incapacity to present itself. The artwork needs external help; it needs an exhibition and a curator to become visible.

Certainly the hidden curatorial practices of contemporary media create the illusion that the images are per se strong and powerful – being able to invade our visual space beyond or even against our explicit consent. These images are presented in the media as 'super-images' endowed with super-natural strength and dynamics. It is these same super-images that are treated by the media as true images, as icons of our time. But the museum curatorial practice undermines this kind of iconophilia, for its medical artifice cannot remain entirely concealed from the viewer. In this respect, museum curating remains unintentionally iconoclastic even as it is programmatically iconophilic. Indeed, curating acts could be seen as a supplement or a pharmacon (in Jacques Derrida's usage) therein that it cures the image even as it makes it unwell. Yet this statement opens the question: what is the right kind of curatorial practice? Since curatorial practice taking place in the museum can never totally conceal itself successfully, the main objective of museal curating must be to visualize itself, by making its practice explicitly visible. Only then the museum can take a stand against the new icons of the popular imagination – in the name of the equal aesthetic rights of all images. The museum can do so effectively by using – we can also say misusing – the artworks as mere illustrations of art history, by recontextualizing images, by problematizing their autonomous status.

Orhan Pamuk's novel, *My Name is Red* features a group of artists searching for a place for art within an iconoclastic culture, namely that of sixteenth century Islamic Turkey. The group are illustrators commissioned by the powerful to ornament their books with exquisite miniatures; subsequently these books are placed in governmental or private collections. Not only are these artists increasingly persecuted by radical Islamic iconoclastic adversaries who want to ban all images; they are also competing against the Occidental painters of the Renaissance, primarily Venetians, who openly affirm their iconophilia. Yet the novel's heroes cannot share this iconophilia, because they do

not believe in the autonomy of images. And so they try to find a way
to take a consistently honest iconoclastic stance, without abandoning
the terrain of art. A Turkish sultan, whose theory of art would actually
serve as good advice for contemporary curatorial practice, shows them
the way. The sultan says the following: '... an illustration that does
not complement a story, in the end, will become but a false idol. Since
we cannot possibly believe in the absent story, we will naturally begin
to believe in the picture itself. This would be no different than the
worship of the idols in the Kaaba that went on before Our Prophet,
peace and blessings be upon him, had destroyed them ... If I believed,
heaven forbid, the way these infidels do, that the Prophet Jesus was
also the Lord God himself, ... only then might I accept the depiction
of mankind in full detail and exhibit such images. You do understand
that, eventually, we would then unthinkingly begin worshipping
any picture that is hung on the wall, don't you?' Orhan Pamuk, My name is Red
(London: Faber and Faber, 2001) 132-133.

This subtle iconoclastic strategy proposed by the sultan – turning
the image back into an illustration – is actually much more effective
than the avant-gardistic strategy. We have known at least since
Magritte that when we look at an image of a pipe, we are not regarding
a real pipe but one that has been painted. The pipe as such is not
there, is not present; instead, it is being depicted as absent. In spite
of this knowledge we are still inclined to believe that when we look
at an artwork, we directly and instantaneously confront 'art'. We see
artworks as incarnating art. The famous distinction between art
and non-art is generally understood as a distinction between objects
inhabited and animated by art, and those from which art is absent.
This is how works of art become art's idols – in an analogous fashion
to religious images, which are also believed to be inhabited or
animated by gods.

To practice the secularization of and by art would mean understanding
artworks not as incarnations of art, but as mere documents, illustrations of art. While they may refer to it, these are nevertheless not
art. To a greater or lesser extent this strategy has been pursued by many
artists since the 1960s. Artistic projects, performances, and actions
have regularly been documented, and by means of this documentation
represented in exhibition spaces and museums. However, such
documentation simply refers to art without itself being art. This type
of documentation is often presented in the framework of an art-
installation for the purpose of narrating a certain project or action.
Traditionally executed paintings, art objects, photographs or videos
can also be utilized in the framework of such installations. In this

case, admittedly, artworks lose their usual status as art. Instead they become documents, illustrations of the story told by the installation. One could say that today's art audience increasingly encounters art documentation, which provides information about the artwork itself, be it an art project or an art action, but in doing so confirms the absence of art in the artwork.

The artist becomes here an independent curator and the independent curator becomes an artist. The independent curator is a radically secularized artist. He is an artist because he does everything artists do. But the independent curator is an artist who has lost the artist's aura, one who no longer has magical powers at his disposal, who cannot endow objects with art's status. He does not use objects – including art objects – for art's sake, but rather abuses them, makes them profane. Yet it is precisely this, which makes the figure of the independent curator so attractive and so essential to the art of today. The contemporary curator is heir apparent to the modern artist, although he does not suffer from his predecessor's magical abnormalities. He is an artist, but atheistic and 'normal' through and through. The curator is an agent of art's profanation, its secularization, its profane abuse.

*Utopia Station* is a good example. Curated by Molly Nesbit, Hans-Ulrich Obrist and Rirkrit Tiravanija, this exhibition was presented at the 50th *Venice Biennale* in 2003. Critical and public discussion of this exhibition focused on whether the concept of utopia is still relevant in this day and age; whether what was put forward as a utopian vision by the curators could really be regarded as such, and so on. Yet, the question concerning whether or not a curatorial project that was clearly iconoclastic could be presented at one of the oldest international art exhibitions seems to me to be far more important than the above considerations. It was iconoclastic because it employed artworks as illustrations, as documents of the search for a social utopia, without emphasizing their autonomous value. It subscribed to the radical iconoclastic approach of the Russian avant-garde, which considered art to be documentation of the search for the 'new man' and towards a 'new life'. Most importantly, though, *Utopia Station* was a curatorial and not an artistic project (even if one of the curators, Rirkrit Tiravanija is an artist). This meant that the iconoclastic gesture could not be accompanied – and thus invalidated – by the attribution of artistic value. Nevertheless it can still be assumed that also in this case the concept of utopia was abused, because it was aestheticized and situated in an elitist art context. And it can equally be said that art was abused as well: it served as an illustration for the curator's vision of utopia. In both cases the spectator had to confront an abuse – be it an abuse of art or by art. Here though, abuse is just another word for iconoclasm.

The space of a museum exhibition or of an artistic installation is often disliked in our days because it is a closed space – contrary to the open space of the contemporary media. But the closure that is effectuated by a museum should not be interpreted as an opposition to 'openness'. By closure the museum creates its outside and opens itself to this outside. The closure is here not an opposition to openness but its precondition. The media space, on the contrary, is not open because it has no outside – it does not want to be open but total, all-inclusive. The art practice that is conceived as a machine of infinite expansion and inclusion is also not an open artwork but an artistic counterpart of an imperial hybris of the contemporary media. The museum exhibition can be made into a place of openness, of disclosure, of unconcealment precisely because it situates inside its finite space, contextualizes, curates images and objects that also circulate in the outside space. In this way it opens itself to its outside. Images do not emerge into the clearing of Being of their own accord, in order for their original visibility to be abused by the 'exhibition business', as Heidegger describes it in his *The Origin of the Work of Art*. It is rather this very abuse that makes them visible.

'… an ideological identification exerts a true hold on us precisely when we maintain an awareness that we are not fully identical to it … For that reason an ideological edifice can be undermined by a too-literal identification.' Slavoj Žižek, *Plague of Phantasies* (London: Verso, 1997) 21-22